About The Author

Ursula Kaiser, owner of Kalkus-Hirco, Inc. has herewith compiled over 100 tart recipes from around the world. Her vast experience in the cookware field and her many contacts throughout the world, enable her to bring you these varied recipes. They are derived from many different ethnic groups and cultures.

At the same time, Ursula will be acquainting you with 2 of her favorite gadgets, the Tartmaster and Krimpkut Sealer. Attractive, delicious appetizers, snacks, lunches, desserts, or even dinners can be prepared easily with these kitchen tools. So, just follow the recipes, and enjoy your Pasta, Pies, and Pastries.

Table of Contents

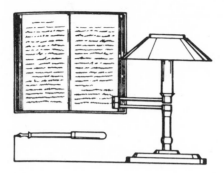

Pasta, Pies, and Pastries

"Tart Recipes From Around The World"

TART MAKING was practiced in ancient Greece as early as the Fifth Century B.C. . Playwright Aristophanes referred in his writings to tarts filled with grapes and almonds and served daintily wrapped in fig leaves. Similar ingredients were used later by the Romans. These recipes that survived from the Fourth Century A.D. included tarts filled with cheese or custard. As time went on, many other countries created their own tart variations. The French made a single crusted large version called a tarte and a small version called a tartelette. The English created a two-crusted pastry which the Americans referred to as a pie. The English also made pasties, small meat filled tarts, which originated as a popular miner's lunch in England's Cornwall. The Spanish prepared empanadas, two-crusted tarts filled with cheese and chilies. The Italians made filled yeast dough calzones, and ravioli using a noodle dough to pocket the meat and cheese fillings. The Polish also used a noodle type dough and filled it with cheese, potatoes, or sauerkraut which were called ed pierogies. Nevertheless, whatever dough was used or whatever filling was added, the basic principles of tart making are and have been an international culinary skill that has been around for centuries.

Now Ursula has added a new dimension to tart making that makes it fun and easy and creates a finished product just like a professional chef's. Presenting the Tartmaster. This simple-to-use gadget cuts, seals, and crimps all at the same time. Just press and twist and like magic before your eyes, you have created tarts, turnovers, bismarks, party sandwiches, snacks for the kids, pastries, pierogies, Chinese dumplings, and many other international favorites. Use your favorite pastry, biscuit, or noodle dough, soft bread, or select puff pastry from your grocer's freezer case. Vary your filling. For desserts: fruits, jams, or custards are good. If you prefer savory fillings for hors d'oeuvres or small entrees use meats, cheeses, vegetables, or combinations of these fillings. Then toast, bake, fry, or deep fry depending on the ingredients you use. The possibilities are endless.

In addition to the Tartmaster, Ursula has simplified the art of pastry decorating by creating the Krimpkut Sealer, a tool essential for practicing a variety of crimping techniques. It not only cuts and crimps, but it also seals at the same time. You can add a variety of shapes to your repetoire of canapes and pastries and create; triangles, rectangles, open crescents, baskets, half moons, and cornucopias. It lets you form ravioli and pierogies in minutes. The dough and fillings can be varied using the Krimpkut Sealer just as suggested with the Tartmaster. Let your imagination go and have fun creating your own combinations.

Both the Tartmaster and the Krimpkut Sealer work together to simplify the art of pastry making, making it an art form that everyone can do, as well as fun for the whole family. Only you will know the secret to your professionally and beautifully prepared party favorites.

Basic Dough Methods

Basic Dough Method for Tarts and Ravioli

Roll out dough in a rectangle. Cut rectangle into two equal parts.

Place filling by teaspoonsful in nicely spaced rows about 2 inches apart on one of the sheets of dough.

Cover with the remaining sheet of dough.

Place the Tartmaster over each mound of filling and press out tarts.

Using the Krimpkut Sealer, cut ravioli in uniform sizes by running the wheel between the mounds of filling.

cook accordingly. . . . then serve

Basic Dough Method for Half-Moons

Roll out dough in a rectangle.

Place filling by teaspoonsful in two nicely spaced rows down the center of the dough leaving a strip of dough along each side, unfilled.

Cover filling with the dough strip on each side.

Cover filling with the dough strip on each side.

Place half of the Tartmaster over each mound of filling and press out half-moons.

cook accordingly. . . . then serve

Basic Dough Method for Cornucopias, Baskets and Open Triangles: Both Large and Small

Using the Krimpkut Sealer cut dough into squares.

Cornucopias: Fold the square in half to form a triangle. Crimp one side together. Fill the open end. Baskets: Place filling in center of square. Overlap two opposite corners of square. Pinch together, firmly.

Open Triangles: Cut square on the diagonal to form two large or four small triangles.

Mini Appetizers:
1. Cut square into four small squares.
2. Crimp or shape as indicated for the large size.

Bake as directed in recipe.

cook accordingly. . . . then serve

Basic Bread Method for Tarts and Ravioli

Place filling by teaspoons-ful in center of bread slice.

Cover filling with second slice of bread.

Place the Tartmaster over mound of filling and press out tart.

Using the Krimpkut Sealer, run the wheel in a square around mound of filling.

cook accordingly. . . . then serve

Closed Bread Triangle

Using the Krimpkut Sealer run the wheel along inside of bread crust to form a square.

Place filling in center on one half of bread square.

Fold other half over filling to form a triangle.

Seal edges with Krimpkut Sealer.

cook accordingly. . . . then serve

Bread Appetizer Shapes

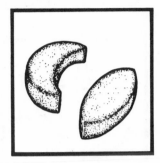

Place the Tartmaster in center of bread slice to press out circle.

Place half the Tartmaster over bread circle.

Press to make crescent and flower petal shapes.

cook accordingly. . . .
then serve

Basic Bread Method for Cornucopias, Baskets and Open Triangles: Both Large and Small

Using the Krimpkut Sealer run the wheel along inside of bread crust to form a square.

A square is used to form the following bread shapes.

Cornucopias: Fold the square in half to form a triangle. Crimp one side together. Fill the open end.

Baskets: Place filling in center of square. Overlap two opposite corners of square. Pinch together, firmly.

Open Triangles: Cut square on the diagonal to form two large or four small triangles.

Mini Cornucopias, Baskets and Triangles:
1. Cut square into four small squares.
2. Crimp or shape as indicated for the large size.

cook accordingly. . . .
then serve

EASY BREAD RECIPES

Attractive tarts, hors d'oeuvres, and tea sandwiches are easy to make and delicious to eat when you start with a simple slice of bread. By varying the filling ingredients and the type of bread used, you can create an unlimited variety of tarts and tea sandwiches using either the Tartmaster or the Krimpkut Sealer. Bread creations can be simple and fun for the whole family if you follow these basic guide lines.

> *Use only fresh bread — white, whole wheat, or rye. The choice is yours.*
>
> *Use either the Tartmaster or the Krimpkut Sealer to seal. Cut, crimp, and seal inside the bread crust.*
>
> *Spoon the filling in the center of the bread leaving a 1/4 inch margin of bread around the edge for a secure seal.*
>
> *When using a moist filling, spread the bread with butter, margarine, or mayonnaise to prevent the bread from getting soggy.*

Select any ingredient or combination of ingredients from the list below, or add your favorite foods chopped or sliced to make your own bread creations.

Any cooked meat, fish	*Pie filling*
or poultry	*Crisp bacon*
Cheese, grated or sliced	*Sauerkraut*
Peanut butter	*Tomatoes*
Hard-boiled egg	*Celery, chopped*
Jam or jelly	*Olives, sliced*
Raisins	*Pickles*
Chopped nuts	*Cream cheese*
Apples	*Avocado*
Pears	*Sauteed mushrooms*
Bananas	*Onion, chopped*
Coconut	*Chocolate chips*
Grated carrot	*Marshmallows*

Bread creations can be served at room temperature, toasted, baked at 375°, sauteed in butter, or deep fried at 365°. They are particularly delicious when dipped in a beaten egg and panfried until lightly browned.

Recipes and suggestion for serving bread creations follow.

Pastry Dough Recipes

BASIC PUFF PASTRY

4 cups all-purpose flour
1 tsp. baking powder
2 tbl. lemon juice plus enough cold water to make 1 cup
2 cups cold butter

1. Sift flour and baking powder onto a very cold work surface and make a well in the center of the flour. Cut 7 tablespoons butter into tiny pieces. Place in center of well. With one hand, begin to draw the flour into the center. Rub in butter until it resembles very fine crumbs. Make a well in the center again. Pour in lemon juice and a little of the cold water.

2. Using 2 knives, work the mixture from the sides to the center, adding a little water from time to time, until a firm but smooth dough is formed. Wrap in waxed paper or foil and refrigerate 30 minutes. Meanwhile, shape remaining butter into a small rectangle and reserve.

3. Roll chilled dough on lightly floured work surface into a narrow rectangle. Place the slab of butter in the center of the dough. Make a parcel of the dough by folding nearest pastry edge into the center of the butter. Fold the sides up and over pressing down gently as you do so. Complete by folding the edge furthest away into the center.

4. Half turn the dough on the work surface. Roll into a narrow rectangle. Wrap and refrigerate 30 minutes.

5. Repeat rolling and folding process 2 more times, refrigerating dough in between. Puff pastry can be refrigerated up to 1 week.

FLAKY PASTRY

3-1/2 cups unbleached all-purpose flour
2 tsp. salt
1-1/4 cup unsalted butter, chilled, cut into 20 pieces
6 tbl. vegetable shortening, chilled
1/4 cup ice water

1. Place half of flour and salt in food processor fitted with steel blade. Add half the butter and shortening. Process until mixture resembles coarse crumbs.

2. With machine running, pour half of the ice water through feed tube. Process until mixture just holds together. Transfer to a lightly floured surface. Repeat with remaining ingredients.

3. Press the 2 patches of dough together. Shape into a ball. Wrap in plastic wrap. Refrigerate 1 hour.

4. Roll pastry into a 12 inch square. Fold into thirds. Roll into a rectangle 21 x 7 inches. Fold it crosswise into thirds. Roll dough into a 12 inch square. Fold into thirds. Wrap in plastic. Refrigerate or freeze until needed.

Makes 3 pounds dough.

PIE CRUST

1-1/2 cups all-purpose flour, sifted
1/2 tsp. salt
Dash of sugar
6 tbl. cold butter, cut into pieces
2 tbl. plus 1 tsp. vegetable shortening
4 to 5 tbl. cold water

1. Combine flour, salt, and sugar in large mixing bowl. Add butter and shortening. Cut into flour with pastry blender or 2 knives until mixture is size of small peas.

2. Add water, 1 tablespoon at a time until mixture forms a ball. Shape into a ball. Wrap in plastic wrap. Refrigerate 30 minutes.

Makes two crust pies

PLAIN DOUGH

3 cups all-purpose flour
3 tbl. olive oil or other good quality oil
1/2 tsp. salt
3/4 cup water

1. Place flour and salt in mixing bowl. Add oil. Work into flour until small particles are formed.

2. Stir in water. Knead well to make a soft dough.

3. Let dough rest for about 15 minutes in a plastic bag or plastic wrap before using.

REFRIGERATOR DOUGH - BASIC RECIPE

1 pkg. active dry yeast
1-1/2 tbl. sugar
1/4 cup warm water (105° to 115°)
3-1/4 cups unbleached all-purpose flour or 3 cups plus 2 tbl. bread flour
1/4 cup unsalted butter, softened
2 tbl. vegetable shortening
1 tsp. salt
2 eggs
1/3 cup cold milk

1. Dissolve yeast in water; add sugar. Place flour, butter, shortening and salt in food processor bowl with metal blade. Process 20 seconds.

2. With machine running, add the eggs and yeast mixture through feed tube. Add milk quickly in a steady stream. Process 30 seconds.

3. Scrape dough into well-greased 3 quart mixing bowl. Cover bowl with oiled plastic wrap. Refrigerate until dough has doubled in bulk, 4 to 6 hours.

4. Punch down dough. If dough is not to be used immediately, cover tightly and refrigerate up to 4 days.

Makes 1-3/4 pounds.

ROUGH PUFF PASTRY

3-1/2 cup sifted all-purpose flour
1 tsp. salt
1 cup butter
3/4 cup vegetable shortening
1 cup ice water

1. Sift flour with salt into mound on working surface. Shape into large ring, forming high wall. Place butter, shortening and half the water in center. Work center mixture together with cutting motion, using 2 knives or pastry scrapers. Work in flour carefully from inside of ring, adding more water as needed. Work with knives until all flour is added and dough holds together.

2. Gather dough into a ball. Chill working surface thoroughly with ice; dust with flour. Roll out pastry into long, thin rectangle. Fold top edge down to center, then bring bottom edge to top fold. Fold bottom to top again, making 5 layers.

3. Turn pastry clockwise 1/2 turn, so edges on left and right area are now at top and bottom. Repeat rolling and folding steps 2 more times. Wrap folded pastry securely in plastic wrap. Store in refrigerator at least 24 hours before using. This pastry will keep in the refrigerator up to 7 days.

SHORTCRUST PASTE

2-1/4 cup all-purpose flour, sifted
1/2 cup plus 2 tbl. butter
1 egg, beaten
1/4 cup milk
1 tsp. salt

1. Rub together flour, butter and salt with fingers until small particles are formed.

2. Stir in egg and milk until mixture forms a ball. Knead lightly. Wrap in plastic wrap. Let rest 1 hour before rolling.

APPETIZERS

CHEESE TURNOVERS

Pastry:

2 cups all purpose flour
1 tsp. salt
1 tsp. baking powder
1 tsp. chili powder
1/2 cup milk
1 egg
1/4 cup butter or margarine, melted
Vegetable oil or shortening for frying

Cheese Filling:

2 tbl. green onion, thinly sliced 2 tbl. parsley, chopped
8 oz. (2 cups) Cheddar or Monterey Jack Cheese, shredded

1. Mix flour, salt, baking powder and chili powder in medium bowl. Combine milk and egg. Stir into flour mixture. Stir in butter. (Dough will be soft.)

2. Turn dough onto lightly floured board. Knead until smooth, about 4 minutes. Shape into a ball. Cover and refrigerate 30 minutes.

3. Cook onion in butter until tender. Remove from heat. Stir in parsley and cheese. Set aside.

4. Divide dough in half. Roll out each half on lightly floured board to 1/8 inch thickness.

5. Cut into circles with large Tartmaster. Place about 1 teaspoon cheese filling in center of each circle. Moisten edges of dough with water. Fold dough over filling to make half-moon shape. Seal edges with Tartmaster or Krimpkut Sealer.

6. Heat oil to 360°. Fry turnovers in oil until golden brown, about 1 minute. Drain on paper toweling. Serve hot.

Makes about 14 appetizers.

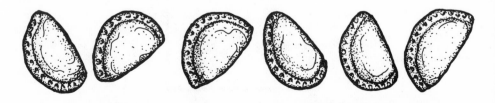

CRAB WONTON
Served with Chinese Mustard Sauce

4 oz. cooked crab meat
1 pkg. (3 oz.) cream cheese, softened
1 tbl. soft bread crumbs
1/4 tsp. sesame seeds
1/4 tsp. seasoned salt
20 to 25 wonton wrappers
Vegetable oil or shortening for frying

Chinese Mustard Sauce:

2 tbl. dry mustard
2 tbl. water

1. Drain and flake crabmeat. Pat dry on paper toweling to remove as much moisture as possible.

2. Combine cream cheese, bread crumbs, sesame seed and seasoned salt. Stir in crabmeat.

3. Place about 1 teaspoon of filling in center of each wonton wrapper. Moisten edges of wrapper with water. Fold 2 opposite corners together, forming a triangle. Seal edges with Krimpkut Sealer.

4. Pull the right and left corners of folded triangle down and below folded edge so they slightly overlap. Moisten overlapping corners and seal with Krimpkut Sealer.

6. Heat oil to 375⁰. Fry wontons a few at a time until golden, 2 to 3 minutes. Drain on paper toweling. Serve hot.

6. For sauce combine mustard and water. Serve with Crab Wonton, if desired.

Makes 20 to 25 appetizers.

CREAMED SPINACH PASTRIES

2 tbl. bacon drippings
About 1 tbl. flour
1 lb. chopped fresh spinach
1 medium grated onion
2 tbl. breadcrumbs
1/2 tsp. salt
1/4 tsp. pepper
1 egg white
1/2 recipe Plain Dough (see page 15)
Vegetable oil or shortening for frying

1. Heat bacon drippings in skillet. Add flour and cook 1 minute. Add spinach to skillet with a little water, the onions and the breadcrumbs. Season with salt and pepper.

2. Cover and steam until spinach is tender. Add the egg white. Stir rapidly to combine.

3. Roll out pastry on lightly floured surface to 1/8 inch thickness. Place spinach filling by tablespoonsful over half of dough, allowing enough room between for cutter.

4. Place remaining half of dough over filling, pressing gently around each mound of filling. Cut into tarts with 3 inch Tartmaster.

5. Heat about 1-1/2 inches oil in large skillet. Pan fry pastries until golden on each side. Drain on paper toweling. Serve warm.

FRIED WONTON

8 oz. uncooked, boneless pork, chicken or turkey
2 tbl. vegetable oil
2 tbl. chopped green onions
4 canned water chestnuts, chopped
1 tbl. dry sherry wine
1/4 tsp. salt
2 tsp. cornstarch
2 tbl. soy sauce
25 to 35 wonton wrappers
Vegetable oil or shortening for frying

1. Finely chop pork. Cook meat in 2 tablespoons oil in skillet 2 to 3 minutes. Add onions, water chesnuts, wine and salt.

2. Dissolve cornstarch in soy sauce. Add to pork mixture. Cook stirring constantly over low heat until thick and translucent.

3. Place about 1 rounded teaspoon of filling in center of each wonton wrapper. Moisten edges of wrapper with water. Fold 2 opposite corners together, forming a triangle. Seal edges with Krimpkut Sealer. Pull the right and left corners of folded triangle down and below folded edge so they slightly overlap. Moisten overlapping corners and seal with Krimpkut sealer.

4. Heat oil to 375⁰. Fry wontons a few at a time until golden, 2 to 3 minutes. Drain on paper toweling. Serve hot.

Makes 25 to 35 appetizers.

HOT MUSHROOM CANAPES

1 lb. mushrooms, finely chopped
1 cup onion, finely chopped
1/4 cup butter or margarine
1/3 cup all-purpose flour
1/3 cup milk
1/2 tsp. salt
1/8 tsp. pepper
30 slices white bread
Freshly grated Parmesan cheese
Sliced stuffed olives

1. Wash mushrooms; dry on paper towels. Chop fine. Saute mushrooms and onion in butter until tender and most of liquid has evaporated. Remove from heat. Stir in flour.

2. Gradually stir in milk; add salt and pepper. Cook, stirring constantly until mixture has thickened. Set aside to cool.

3. Using a 3 inch Tartmaster, cut bread into rounds. Spread with mushroom mixture, using about 1 tablespoon for each. Arrange in a single layer on tray.

4. Sprinkle with a little Parmesan cheese. Freeze until firm. Remove to foil tray; freezer-wrap and seal. Store in freezer until serving.

5. To serve, arrange frozen canapes on cookie sheets. Broil, about 8 inches from source of heat 5 minutes or until brown. Garnish each with olive slice.

Makes 30.

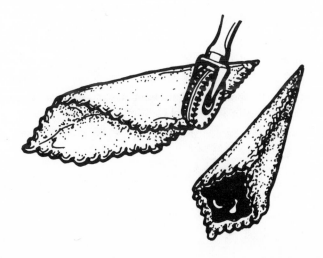

LAMB AND CURRY APPETIZERS

Pastry:

2 cups all-purpose flour
2/3 cup shortening
1/2 teaspoon curry powder
3/4 tsp. salt
1/4 tsp. pepper
1/4 to 1/3 cup cold water
Milk

Filling:

8 oz. ground lamb
1/2 cup chopped onion
1/2 cup chopped, peeled apple
1/3 cup plain yogurt
2 tsp. curry powder
1/4 tsp. salt

1. Combine flour, curry powder, salt and pepper. Cut in shortening until size of small peas. Add enough water to form a dough. Shape dough into ball. Cover and refrigerate 30 minutes.

2. Cook lamb and onion until meat browns. Drain off fat. Stir in remaining filling ingredients. Cool Slightly.

3. Heat oven to 375⁰. Divide dough in half. Roll each half on lightly floured surface to 1/8 inch thickness. Cut into 3 inch rounds with Tartmaster. Re-roll dough as necessary.

4. Place 1 heaping teaspoons of filling in center of each round; fold into half-moon shapes. Seal edges with Tartmaster or Krimpkut Sealer.

5. Place on baking sheets. Brush with milk. Bake at 375⁰ until golden, about 15 minutes.

Makes 24 appetizers.

MINI CHICKEN-ALMOND TURNOVERS

Pastry:

1 cup all-purpose flour
1/2 tsp. salt
2/3 cup heavy cream
Vegetable oil or shortening for frying

Chicken-Almond Filling:

1 can (4-3/4 oz.) chicken spread
2 tbl. chopped blanched almonds
1 hard-cooked egg, peeled, chopped
1 tbl. bacon bits

1. Combine flour and salt. Stir in enough of the cream to make a stiff dough.

2. Combine chicken-almond filling ingredients.

3. Roll out dough on lightly floured board to 1/8 inch thickness. Cut dough into 3 inch circles with small Tartmaster. Place about 1 teaspoon chicken-almond filling in center of each circle. Fold dough over to make half-moon shapes. Seal with Krimpkut Sealer.

4. Heat oil to 375°. Fry turnovers until golden, 1-1/2 to 2 minutes. Drain on paper toweling. Serve hot.

Makes 30 appetizers.

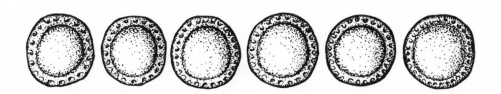

MUSHROOM CRESCENTS

4 pkgs. (3 oz. each) cream cheese, at room temperature
1/2 cup plus 2 tbl. unsalted butter, softened
1-1/2 cups all-purpose flour
1 medium onion, finely chopped
1/2 lb. mushrooms, chopped
1/2 tsp. dried thyme
1 egg, lightly beaten with 1 teaspoon water

1. Place 3 packages cream cheese and 1/2 cup of the butter in food processor bowl fitted with steel blade. Process 1 minute, stopping twice to scrape down bowl.

2. Add flour, 1/2 cup at a time using on/off motion until flour is absorbed. Remove dough. Flatten into a disc. Wrap in plastic. Refrigerate 30 minutes.

3. Melt remaining 2 tbl. butter in skillet over high heat. Add onion and cook, stirring often until onion is lightly browned.

4. Add mushrooms and cook, stirring until the moisture from the mushrooms has evaporated, about 5 minutes. Stir in remaining cream cheese until mixed. Stir in thyme and pepper to taste. Remove pan from heat. Cool mixture to room temperature.

5. Roll out pastry half at a time on lightly floured surface to 1/8 inch thickness. Cut out rounds with 3 inch Tartmaster. Reroll dough as necessary.

6. Place about 1 teaspoon filling in center of each round. Fold dough over filling to form half-moon shape. Press edges with Tartmaster.

7. Place on ungreased baking sheet. Brush tops with egg mixture. Make 2 small slits in top of each crescent. Bake in preheated 400° oven until golden, about 15 minutes. Cool slightly. Serve warm.

Makes about 4-1/2 dozen.

Note: Cooled crescents may be frozen and reheated at 300° for 20 minutes.

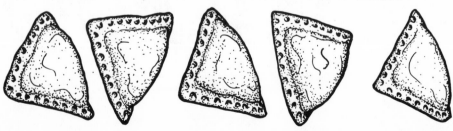

MUSHROOM HAM CRISPS

32 large, firm mushrooms
1/4 cup butter or margarine
1 can (4-1/2 oz.) devilled ham
1-1/2 tsp. prepared mustard
1 pkg. (17-1/4 oz.) puff pastry

1. Wash mushrooms gently. Remove stems and reserve for another use.

2. Saute mushroom caps in butter until almost tender. Remove from skillet; drain on paper toweling.

3. Combine ham and mustard.

4. Thaw puff pastry sheets 20 minutes; unfold. Heat oven to 425°. Roll each sheet on a lightly floured surface to an 11 inch square. Cut each square into 16 smaller squares with Krimpkut Sealer.

5. Fill mushroom caps evenly with ham mixture. Place one filled cap, filled side down, in center of each pastry square. Brush edges with water. Bring corners of pastry together to enclose mushroom completely. Seal with Krimpkut sealer.

6. Place seam-side down on ungreased baking sheet. Bake until golden, 12 to 15 minutes. Serve hot.

Makes 32.

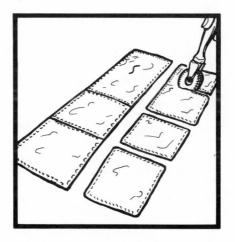

MUSHROOM TARTS

12 mushrooms, chopped
1 green onion (with 2 inches of green) minced
1/2 cup whipping cream
Pinch of dried tarragon
Salt
Freshly ground pepper
Basic puff pastry, (Reference Page 13)
1 egg yolk

1. Combine mushrooms, onion, cream and tarragon in heavy skillet. Cook over medium-high heat, stirring occasionally, until cream is thickened, about 10 to 15 minutes. Season with salt and pepper. Cool.

2. Roll out pastry on lightly floured surface as thin as possible. Cut into 3-inch squares.

3. Place about 1 teaspoon filling in center of each square. Fold dough over to form a triangle. Seal with Krimpkut Sealer.

4. Place on ungreased baking sheet. Brush with egg yolk. Bake in preheated 400° oven until golden, 12 to 15 minutes.

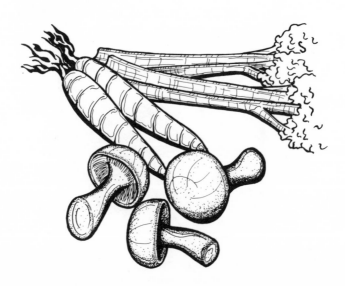

SOUTH-OF-THE-BORDER WONTON

1/2 lb. lean ground beef
1 green onion, finely chopped
1/2 tsp. salt
1/2 tsp. chili powder
1/4 tsp. garlic salt
1/2 cup grated Monterey Jack cheese
2 tbl. minced ripe olives
30 to 35 wonton wrappers
Vegetable oil or shortening for frying

1. Cook beef in skillet until brown; drain excess fat. Add onion and cook until tender. Stir in salt, chili powder, garlic salt, cheese and olives. Cool mixture slightly.

2. Place about 1 teaspoon filling in center of each wonton wrapper. Moisten edges of wrapper with water. Fold 2 opposite corners together, forming a triangle. Seal edges with Krimpkut Sealer.

3. Pull the right and left corners of folded triangle down and below folded edges so they slightly overlap. Moisten overlapping corners and seal with Krimpkut Sealer.

4. Heat oil to 375°. Fry wontons a few at a time until golden, 2 to 3 minutes.

   Drain on paper toweling. Serve hot.

Makes 30 to 35 appetizers.

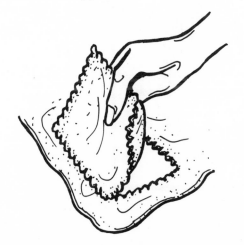

SPINACH ROLLS

1/2 lb. fresh spinach (with stems) rinsed and dried
1 pkg. (8 oz.) cream cheese, cut into 4 pieces
2 large green onions, cut into 1-inch pieces
1 egg
1 oz. Bleu cheese (about 1/4 cup)
2 slices white bread, torn into 4 pieces
1/2 tsp. salt
1/4 tsp. freshly grated nutmeg
1/2 tsp. freshly ground pepper
3 oz. Westphalian, Black Forest or other smoked and cured ham, diced
White bread slices

1. Place all ingredients except ham and sliced bread in bowl of food processor fitted with steel blade. Process 30 seconds, stopping once to scrape down sides of work bowl. Add ham and mix 3 seconds.

2. Place about 1 tablespoon filling in center of each bread slice. Top with another bread slice. Cut and seal with Tartmaster. Toast or deep fry as desired.

TUNA PICKUPS

1 tbl. butter or margarine
1 tbl. flour
1/3 cup milk
1/4 tsp. salt
1 can (6-1/4 oz.) tuna, drained
2 tbl. diced pimiento
1/2 cup chopped ripe olives
Dash liquid hot pepper seasoning
Pie pastry for 2-crust pie
Heavy cream

1. Melt butter in saucepan. Stir in flour. Heat until bubbly. Stir in milk and salt. Cook, stirring constantly until thickened.

2. Remove from heat. Stir in tuna, onion, pimiento, olives and hot pepper seasoning.

3. Roll out pastry on lightly floured board to 1/16 inch thickness. Cut into 2 inch squares with Krimpkut Sealer.

4. Place 1 rounded teaspoon filling in center of each square. Bring two opposite corners of pastry together over filling. Seal with Krimpkut Sealer. Refrigerate.

5. Heat oven to 450⁰. Place pastries on ungreased baking sheet. Brush with cream.

Bake until golden, about 10 minutes.

Serve hot.

TUNA WONTON

1 can tuna in oil (6-1/2 oz.), drained, flaked
8 canned water chestnuts, finely chopped
2 green onions, chopped
1 tbl. soy sauce
1/2 tsp. sugar
1 egg, beaten
30 to 35 wonton wrappers
Vegetable oil or shortening for frying

1. Combine tuna, water chestnuts, onions, soy sauce, sugar and egg.

2. Place about 1 teaspoon of filling in center of each wonton wrapper. Moisten edges of wrapper with water. Fold 2 opposite corners together, forming a triangle. Seal edges with Krimpkut Sealer.

3. Pull the right and left corners of folded triangle down and below folded edge so they slightly overlap. Moisten overlapping corners and seal with Krimpkut Sealer.

4. Heat oil to 375°. Fry wontons a few at a time until golden, 2 to 3 minutes. Drain on paper toweling. Serve hot.

Makes 30 to 35 appetizers.

TYROPETES

4 green onions, finely chopped
5 oz. ricotta or farmer's cheese
2 tsp. fennel seed
5 oz. cream cheese at room temperature
1 cup crumbled Feta cheese
3 tbl. minced parsley
1 egg, well beaten
Basic (Page 13) or Frozen Puff Pastry

1. Combine onion, cheeses, parsley and fennel until smooth. Stir in egg.

2. Roll out pastry on lightly floured surface to 1/8 inch thickness. Cut into 3 inch squares with Krimpkut Sealer.

3. Place about 1-1/2 teaspoons filling in center of each square. Fold into triangles. Seal with Krimpkut Sealer.

4. Place pastries on ungreased baking sheet. Brush with egg. Bake in preheated 400° oven, 15 to 20 minutes.

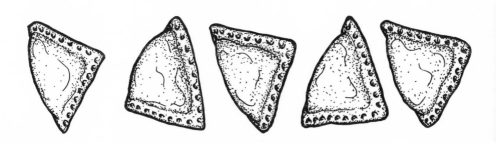

Favorite Appetizer Fillings

The following fillings can be used with either fresh bread; white, whole wheat or rye or any of the pastry recipes in this book. If using pastry or dough, prepare the pastry or dough and the filling as directed. Spoon the filling between 2 sheets of dough. Using the Tartmaster cut and seal for individual tarts. For crescent and petal shapes, cut the tart in half using the Tartmaster. For turnovers, baskets, cornucopias, and squares use the Krimpkut Sealer. Bake at 375° for 10-12 minutes or deep-fat fry at 365° until golden.

If using bread, prepare the filling as directed. Butter the inner sides of 2 bread slices. Spoon the filling between the slices. Use the Tartmaster or Krimpkut Sealer as indicated above for pastry or dough. If making open-faced bread appetizers, serve slightly chilled, toasted, or bake at 350° until lightly browned. If filling is enclosed, serve bread appetizers as directed for open-faced appetizers. For variety deep fry at 365° until golden or dip in a beaten egg and saute in melted butter until crisp and lightly browned.

The appetizer variations are unlimited. Combine any of the fillings or add your favorite filling with a special bread or dough of your choice and create your own unique appetizers.

CRAB FILLING

1 tbl. vegetable oil
1/2 medium onion, chopped
1 small garlic clove, minced
6 oz. cooked or canned crab, drained, flaked
3 Spanish-style green olives, pitted, chopped

Saute onion and garlic in oil until tender. Stir in remaining ingredients. Cook over medium heat 3 to 5 minutes. Cool.

CRAB APPETIZERS

1 pkg. (3 oz.) cream cheese, at room temperature
2 tbl. sour cream
2 tsp. dry sherry
1/2 tsp. salt
2 tsp. capers
1/2 tsp. poppy seeds
1 can (6-1/2 oz.) crabmeat, drained and flaked

In a medium bowl, combine cream cheese, sour cream and sherry. Stir in remaining ingredients.

CRAB IMPERIAL FILLING

1 green pepper, minced
1 medium onion, minced
2 tsp. dry mustard
2 tsp. prepared horseradish
2 tsp. salt
1/2 tsp. freshly ground white pepper
2 eggs, beaten
1 cup mayonnaise
3 lb. crab meat lumps
Paprika

1. Combine the green pepper, onion, mustard, horseradish, salt, white pepper and eggs. Stir in mayonnaise. Fold in the crabmeat.

SALMON FILLING

1 7-3/4 oz. can red salmon, or crabmeat, well-drained
1/4 cup mayonnaise
4 drops hot sauce
1/4 tsp. dry mustard
Salt and pepper to taste
1 pkg. (3 oz.) cream cheese, softened
2 tsp. lemon juice
1 tsp. finely minced green onion
1/4 tsp. curry powder

Flake the salmon with a fork; remove bones. Combine all ingredients until smooth. Refrigerate overnight before using.

This makes about 1-1/4 cups filling.

LOBSTER FILLING

1 pkg. (3 oz.) cream cheese, softened
1 cup diced, cooked lobster
1 tbl. mayonnaise
1/2 tsp. capers
2 tsp. lemon juice
Salt and pepper to taste

Combine all ingredients. Refrigerate before using.

SPICY HAM FILLING

2/3 cup minced green onions
2 tbl. butter
2 garlic cloves, minced
1 tsp. grated fresh ginger
1/2 cup minced fresh red pepper
1/2 cup minced fennel or celery
1/2 cup minced ham
2 tbl. butter

On low heat, saute green onions, garlic and ginger in 2 tablespoons butter until tender but not brown, about 4 to 5 minutes. Raise heat to medium-heat, add red pepper and fennel. Cook stirring constantly, about 3 minutes. Add ham and mix well.

PECAN-CHICKEN SALAD FILLING

3 cups finely diced cooked chicken
1 cup minced celery
1/2 cup ground pecans
1/3 cup Mayonnaise
1 tsp. salt
1/8 tsp. onion salt
1 tbl. lemon juice
1/4 cup sour cream

Combine the chicken, celery and pecans. Stir in the remaining ingredients. Chill thoroughly.

Lunches

BASIC RAVIOLI

Dough:
3-1/3 cups sifted all-purpose flour
1 tbl. salt
4 eggs
1 tbl. olive oil
4 to 5 tbl. water

1. Brown salt pork in butter and oil in skillet. Add onions; saute until golden.

2. Remove casing from sausage. Add sausage, beef and livers to skillet. Cook slowly, stirring constantly, 15 minutes. Stir in remaining ingredients. Cook 10 minutes longer. Cool. Force mixture through food grinder twice. Refrigerate filling until ready to use.

3. Sift flour and salt and mound onto a large board. Make a well in the center. Place eggs, oil and half the water in well.

4. Beat egg mixture in well with a fork until smooth. Gradually work in flour with egg mixture until a firm, but not dry dough as formed. Add more water if necessary. Knead dough on floured board until smooth. Shape into a ball. Cover and let rest 30 minutes.

5. Divide dough into 2 parts. Roll each half on lightly floured board until very thin.

6. Place desired filling by teasponnsful in nicely spaced rows about 2 inches apart on one of the sheets. Cover with remaining sheet of dough. using Kimpkut Sealer, cut out ravioli in uniform sizes by running the wheel between the mounds.

7. Drop ravioli into boiling chicken broth or lightly salted water. Cook until tender, 5 to 10 minutes. Drain, serve with tomato sauce and grated cheese.

Beef Filling:
1/3 cup diced salt pork
2 tbl. butter
2 tbl. olive oil
1-1/2 cup chopped onion
1/2 lb. mild Italian sausage
3/4 lb. lean ground beef
1/4 cup chopped chicken livers
1 bay leaf
1 clove garlic, crushed
Salt and freshly ground pepper
1 can (1 lb.) tomatoes, drained, chopped
1 tbl. tomato paste

CALIFORNIA TEA TART

Avocado, sliced thin
Swiss or Monterey Jack cheese, shredded
Alfalfa sprouts
Mayonnaise
Whole wheat bread

Spread the center of one slice of whole wheat bread with mayonnaise. Add sliced avocado and shredded cheese. Top with alfalfa sprouts. Cover with a second slice of bread. Cut and seal with the Tartmaster. Toast until lightly browned.

CHEESE TARTS

3 cups dry cottage cheese
2 egg yolks, beaten
1/4 cup sugar
1 tbl. butter, melted
1/2 tsp. salt
1/2 tsp. cinnamon
Plain dough (see recipe page 15)
Vegetable oil or shortening for frying

1. Combine all ingredients for filling.

2. Roll out pastry on lightly floured surface to 1/8 inch thickness. Place cheese filling by tablespoons over half of dough, allowing enough room between for cutter.

3. Place remaining half of dough over filling, pressing gently around each mound of filling. Cut into tarts with 3 inch Tartmaster.

4. Heat about 1-1/2 inches of oil in large skillet. Pan fry pastries until golden on each side. Drain on paper toweling. Serve warm or cold, sprinkle with confectioners' sugar.

CHEESY MEAT SANDWICHES

1/4 cup butter or margarine, softened
1 tsp. prepared horseradish
8 slices white, whole wheat or rye bread
1 cup chopped cooked ham, beef or other leftover meat
4 oz. whipped cream cheese with chives
1/4 cup chopped water chestnuts
2 tbl. sweet pickle relish, well-drained
2 tbl. milk

1. Combine butter and horseradish. Spread 4 slices of bread with the mixture.

2. Combine meat, cream cheese, water chestnuts, relish and milk. Spoon about 1/3 cup mixture on buttered bread slices. Top with remaining bread slices. Cut and seal with Tartmaster.

3. Sandwiches can be wrapped and frozen for up to 2 weeks.

Makes 4 sandwiches.

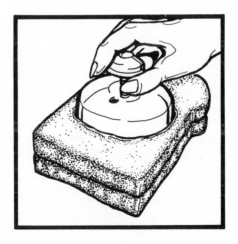

CHICKEN HAND PIES

2 slices bacon, cut into 1/2 inch pieces
1 cup boiling water
3 chicken thighs, skinned, boned and cut into 1/2 inch pieces
1/4 cup diced carrot
3 tbl. finely chopped onion
1 tbl. minched parsley
1/8 tsp. pepper
1 package (10 oz.) piecrust mix (enough for two 9" pies)
1 egg beaten with 1 tbl. water

1. Add bacon to boiling water; boil 10 minutes. Drain. Combine bacon, chicken, carrot, onion, parsley and pepper.

2. Prepare pastry according to package directions. Roll dough out on floured surface into a rectangle 12 x 7 inches. Cut out four 6-inch circles of pastry. Press scraps of dough together. Reroll and cut out one more circle.

3. Spoon some of filling on bottom half of each circle. Spread to within 3/4 inch of the edge. Brush edge of pastry with water. Fold top half of pastry over filling to form a crescent shape. Crimp edges with Krimpkut Sealer, making sure filling is enclosed.

4. Place pies on baking sheet lined with aluminum foil. Brush pies with egg mixture. Using a fork or small knife, poke steam vents in top of each pie.

5. Bake pies in preheated 425° oven 10 minutes. Reduce temperature to 375°. Bake until golden 20 to 25 minutes longer. Baked pies can be frozen. To reheat, bake pies at 325° for 30 to 40 minutes.

Makes 5 pies.

CORNISH BEEF PASTIES

    1 recipe basic pastry (reference page)
1 cup finely diced potatoes
1 cup finely diced rutabaga
8 ounces ground round steak
1/4 cup minced onion
Salt and freshly ground pepper to taste
1 egg, slightly beaten

1. Cook potatoes and rutabagas in boiling salted water separately until crisp-tender; drain.

2. Roll out pastry on lightly floured surface to thickness of 1/8 inch. Cut six 6-inch circles from the pastry.

3. Combine potatoes and rutabaga. Place 1/6 of the mixture on half of each pastry circle leaving a 1/2 inch edge to seal. Combine beef, onion, salt and pepper. Spread evenly over the potato mixture on each circle.

4. Moisten edges of pastry with water. Fold top half of pastry over filling to form a crescent shape. Crimp edges of pasties with Krimpkut Sealer.

5. Place on greased baking sheet, sealed edges up. Brush pasties with egg. Bake in preheated 400° oven 10 minutes. Reduce temperature to 350°. Bake until golden brown, about 25 minutes longer.

Makes 6 pasties.

CORNISH MEAT PIES

1/2 lb. lean ground beef
1/2 lb. lean ground pork
2 tbl. chopped onion
2 tbl. flour
2 tbl. minced parsley
1-1/2 tsp. sage leaves, crumbled
1/2 tsp. salt
1/4 tsp. pepper
1/2 tsp. ground allspice
1 cup heavy cream
1 cup cooked potatoes, peeled and finely diced
1 cup diced, cored and peeled apples mixed with 2 tbl. light brown sugar
1 pkg. (17-1/4 oz.) frozen puff pastry
1 egg, beaten with 1 tbl. water

1. In a large skillet, saute beef, pork and onion for 3 to 5 minutes or until meat is browned and onion is soft. Drain fat. Sprinkle flour over meat in skillet. Cook 1 minute longer, stirring constantly.

2. Add parsley, sage, salt, pepper, allspice and cream; cook, stirring 1 to 2 minutes or until mixture thickens.

3. Add potatoes and apple-sugar mixture and cook 1 minute longer. Cool mixture completely.

4. Thaw puff pastry 20 minutes at room temperature. Gently unfold, being careful not to crack. On a lightly floured surface, roll one sheet to a 16 inch square. Put about 3 tbl. meat filling about 6 inches apart on pastry. Roll out other half of pastry and cover over fillings. Cut with 4 inch Tartmaster.

5. Brush with glaze. Place pies on an ungreased baking sheet. Bake in 400° preheated oven for 12 to 16 minutes or until puffed and golden. Serve warm or at room temperature.

CRAB PUFFS

4 egg whites at room temperature
3/4 tsp. cream of tartar
1-1/4 cups mayonnaise
8 ounces flaked crabmeat
1 tbl. chives
1/2 tbl. freshly ground pepper
1/2 tbl. ground red pepper
16 slices bread
Paprika for garnish

1. Beat egg whites in large bowl until foamy. Add cream of tartar and continue beating until very stiff. Combine mayonnaise, crabmeat, chives and pepper. Fold into egg whites. Trim crusts from bread and halve diagonally with Krimpkut Sealer; toast.

2. Arrange toast triangles on large baking sheet. Top each piece with 1 heaping tablespoon crab mixture. Sprinkle with paprika. Broil 4 to 5 inches from heat source until puffed and golden brown, about 2 to 5 minutes.
Serve immediately.

Makes 32.

FRIED MOZZARELLA SANDWICHES

8 slices soft white bread
4 slices Mozzarella cheese
3 eggs
Enough oil or melted butter to cover bottom of large skillet

1. Cut the crusts off the bread and put one slice of cheese between each 2 slices of bread.

2. Pinch the edges together to seal the cheese inside using the Krimpkut Sealer. Beat the eggs in a shallow dish; soak the sandwiches in the eggs and fry quickly in a skillet of hot oil or melted butter. Fry until lightly browned on both sides.

Makes 4 servings.

HAM AND CHEESE FLORENTINE

1 sheet frozen puff pastry
1 cup spinach, chopped
2 slices boiled ham
2 slices turkey
Salt and pepper
1/3 cup Gruyere or Swiss cheese, grated
1 egg, beaten

1. Thaw folded pastry sheet 20 minutes; unfold gently. Cut pastry into 4 squares with Krimpkut Sealer. On a lightly floured board, roll out each pastry square 1" longer and 1" wider.

2. Place spinach evenly on 2 pastry squares. Top with ham and turkey slices. Sprinkle with salt, pepper and grated cheese.

3. Top with 2 remaining pastry squares. Seal edges with Krimpkut Sealer. Brush pastry with beaten egg. Pierce tops of pastry. Place on ungreased baking sheet. Bake in preheated 350° oven for 30 minutes.

Makes 2 servings.

ITALIAN CALZONES

Dough:
1 pkg. active dry yeast
1/2 cup warm water (105° to 115°)
4 cups unbleached all-purpose flour
1 tsp. salt
Warm water as needed

Filling:
6 oz. Italian hard salami, diced
12 oz. Mozzarella cheese, shredded
Olive oil
1 egg, beaten with a little water

1. Dissolve yeast in 1/2 cup warm water. Let stand in warm place until bubbly. Put flour in a 4 to 5 quart mixing bowl with the salt. Stir to combine. Make a well in the flour. Add the yeast mixture. Work the flour into the liquid in the center. Add warm water 1/4 cup at a time until you have a soft dough that cleans the sides of the mixing bowl.

2. Turn the dough onto a lightly floured surface. Knead the dough for 5 to 6 minutes or until it is smooth. Lightly flour a 4 to 5 quart mixing bowl and the ball of dough. Place the dough in the bowl. Cover the bowl with plastic wrap and a towel.

3. Let dough rise in a warm place about 1 to 1-1/2 hours or until doubled in bulk.

4. Remove dough from mixing bowl; knead about 2 minutes. Divide the dough into 6 equal pieces. On a lightly floured surface, roll each piece into a circle that is 8 to 9 inches in diameter and about 1/8 inch thick.

5. Brush the surface lightly with olive oil. In the center of each circle, put an even amount of salami and cheese. Moisten the edges of each circle with the beaten egg. Fold the dough over onto itself to form a half circle. Cut and seal with Krimpkut Sealer. Brush the outside of each calzone with a small amount of olive oil.

6. Set them on a baking sheet. Cover with a towel and set them in a warm place for 1 hour. Bake the calzone in a preheated 375° oven for about 30 minutes or until golden brown.

KNOEDELN
(Fruit Filled Potato Dumplings)

2 lbs. cooked potatoes
2-2/4 to 3 cups all-purpose flour
1 tsp. salt
1 egg
2 lbs. prune plums, halved, or fried prunes, pitted
1/2 cup butter
8 tbl. bread crumbs
1 tbl. ground cinnamon

1. Drain potatoes and mash. Add flour, salt and egg. Mix until dough is formed. Cover and refrigerate 30 minutes.

2. Divide dough in half. Roll out each half on lightly floured surface to 1/4 inch thickness. Arrange plums on half of dough, about 2 inches apart. Sprinkle plums with sugar.

3. Top with second half of dough. Using Krimpkut Sealer or Tartmaster, cut out Knoedeln in uniform sizes by running the wheel between the mounds.

4. Drop Knoedeln in boiling salted water. Simmer 10 minutes; drain well. Melt butter in skillet. Add breadcrumbs. Sprinkle over Knoedeln. Serve with cottage cheese, sugar and cinnamon.

LITTLE HAM PASTRIES

1/2 cup ground ham
1 egg
1 tbl. sour cream
Pinch of white pepper
1/4 tsp. dried tarragon
1 egg yolk, beaten
Five-minute puff pastry, (Reference Page)

1. Mix ham, whole egg, sour cream, pepper and tarragon.

2. Roll out pastry on lightly floured surface as thin as possible. Cut into 3-inch squares.

3. Place 1/2 teaspoon filling in center of each square. Fold dough over filling to form a triangle. Seal with Krimpkut Sealer.

4. Place on ungreased baking sheet. Brush with egg yolk. Bake in preheated 400° oven until golden, 12 to 15 minutes.

LOBSTER ORIENTAL PUFFS

1 lb. lobster meat
1 tbl. salad oil
1 can (8 oz.) sliced mushrooms, drained
1 clove garlic
1/2 cup diced celery
1/2 cup diced bamboo shoots
1/2 cup diced water chestnuts
1 cup peapods
1 tsp. cornstarch
1/2 tsp. sugar
1/2 tsp. salt
1 tsp. soy sauce
1/2 cup chicken broth
3/4 cup cashews
Plain dough (see recipe page   )
Vegetable oil

1. Cut lobster into 1 inch pieces. Heat oil in skillet; saute garlic and remove. Saute lobster 30 seconds. Add mushrooms, celery, bamboo shoots, water chestnuts and peapods. Stir fry 30 seconds.

2. Mix cornstarch with sugar, salt, soy sauce and broth; stir into vegetable mixture. Simmer, stirring constantly, until sauce thickens; quickly stir in cashews.

3. Roll out pastry half at a time on lightly floured surface to thickness of 1/8 inch. Place filling in mounds over 1/2 dough allowing room between for cutter.

4. Brush edges of dough with water. Place remaining half of dough over the meat, pressing gently around each mound. Seal and cut into rounds with Tartmaster.

5. Heat about 1 inch oil in skillet. Fry puffs until golden on each side. Drain on paper toweling. Serve warm.

MINI-PIROSHKI

Cream Cheese Pastry:
1/2 cup butter, softened
4 oz. cream cheese, softened
1 cup all-purpose flour
Dash salt

Filling:
1 medium onion, finely chopped
1 tbl. butter
About 5 oz. lean ground beef
1/4 tsp. salt
Freshly ground pepper
1/2 tsp. dried dill
1 hard cooked egg, finely chopped
Plain yogurt

1. Cream butter and cheese. Beat in flour and salt. Shape into a ball; sprinkle with flour. Cover with plastic wrap; refrigerate 1 hour.

2. For Filling: Saute onion in butter. Add beef. Cook until brown. Drain excess fat. Add seasonings and egg. Let cool slightly. If mixture appears dry, add 1 to 2 tablespoons yogurt.

3. Roll out dough on lightly floured surface to 1/8 inch thickness. Cut into 3 inch rounds with Tartmaster. Place about 1 teaspoon filling on each circle. Fold dough over filling to form a half-moon.

4. Seal edges using Tartmaster. Pierce tops of pastries with fork. Place on ungreased baking sheet. Bake in preheated 400° oven until golden, about 15 minutes. Serve with sour cream or yogurt mixed with a little dried dill.

Makes 24 pastries.

PIEROGI

7 to 8 cups all-purpose flour, sifted
1 tsp. salt (or to taste)
6 egg yolks
1-1/2 cups milk
1/2 oz. butter, melted
Butter
Garnish

Note: Dough has a tendency to dry while you are working, and dry dough will not seal properly. To prevent this, place a very moist towel over dough. Place uncooked Pierogi in a shallow pan before boiling; do not crowd or pile or they will stick.

1. Pour flour into a large mixing bowl, or mound on large board. Make a deep well in the center. Place salt, egg yolks, milk and butter in well. Working with your fingertips or a large spoon, slowly mix the flour into the liquid ingredients. Mix vigorously until dough is stiff enough to be gathered into a compact ball. If dough is crumbly, add additional milk by the teaspoon.

2. Knead until dough is firm, about 10 minutes. Let dough rest, about 10 minutes.

3. Divide dough into 4 parts. Roll each part on lightly floured surface as thin as possible, about 1/8 inch thick. Cut into rounds with 4 inch Tartmaster.

4. Place 1 tablespoon filling in center of each circle. Fold dough over filling to make half-moon shape. Seal edges with Krimpkut Sealer. Gather scraps of dough and roll into additional circles. Continue rolling and filling until all dough is used.

5. Bring 4 quarts of salted water to a boil in a 5 to 6 quart pot. Drop in Pierogi. Simmer dumplings uncovered, 5 to 10 minutes or until they rise to surface of water. Remove with slotted spoon and transfer to a heated platter. Pierogi are served with melted butter drizzled over or they can be pan fried in butter until golden brown. Onion or dry breadcrumbs can be added to the butter for additional flavor. Serve Pierogi with side dish or garnish of chopped dill or parsley, breadcrumbs or sour cream.

Makes 3 to 4 dozen.

Cheese Filling:

1 lb. dry, large-curd cottage cheese or bakers cheese
1/2 tsp. salt
1 tsp. lemon juice
1 tbl. sugar
2 eggs
2 egg yolks

1. Puree cheese in food mill or force through sieve with back of spoon. Beat in other ingredients until thoroughly mixed.

Provides filling for about 32 Pierogi.

Cherry Filling:

3 lbs. fresh sour cherries, pitted, or substitute 3 cups drained, canned, pitted sour cherries
1/3 cup sugar

1. Combine fruit and sugar in 2-quart enameled or stainless saucepan. Heat to boiling; reduce heat, simmer 3 to 5 minutes.
2. With a slotted spoon, transfer cherries to a small bowl. Heat the juices remaining in the pan to boiling. Boil uncovered for 2 to 3 minutes, or until mixture thickens into a light syrup.
3. Pour the syrup into a small bowl and set aside. When Pierogi are served, pour light syrup over.

Provides filling for about 32 Pierogi.

POLISH LINKS

1-1/2 cups all-purpose flour
1 package (3 oz.) cream cheese, softened
1/2 cup butter
6 Polish links
1 egg yolk, beaten

1. Combine flour, cream cheese and butter; mix until a soft dough forms. Roll out dough. With Krimpkut Sealer, divide dough into 7 equal parts. Wrap each link in dough. Brush with beaten egg.

2. Cut remaining dough into crescent shapes with Krimpkut Sealer. Place crescents on top of pastry. Brush with egg. Bake in preheated 425° oven 10 to 12 minutes or until golden brown. Slice to serve.

Makes 6 servings.

SCALLOPS AND MUSHROOMS IN PASTRY

1 lb. scallops
1/2 lb. mushrooms, sliced
2 tbl. butter
1/3 cup half-and-half
1 tbl. flour
2 tbl. Sauterne wine
1/4 cup minced parsley
1 tsp. salt
1/2 tsp. freshly ground pepper
1 recipe Rough Puff Pastry (see recipe page 17)
1 egg, beaten with 1 tbl. water

1. Cut large scallops in quarters. Saute scallops and mushrooms in butter until almost tender. Combine half-and-half, flour, wine, parsley, salt and pepper. Add to scallop mixture.

2. Cook until thickened. Cool mixture. Roll out pastry on lightly floured surface to 1/8 inch thickness. Cut into 5 inch squares. Using Krimpkut Sealer.

3. Place small amount of filling on half of pastry. Brush a little egg mixture on edges of pastry. Fold dough over filling to form a triangular shape. Seal edges with Krimpkut Sealer. Place pastries on dampened baking sheet. Brush with egg mixture. Bake in preheated 425° oven until golden, about 25 minutes.

SPICY RICOTTA TURNOVERS

Dough:
1/2 cup whole wheat flour
1 cup all-purpose flour
1/2 tsp. salt
6 tbl. butter, softened
1 egg, lightly beaten
3 tbl. milk

Filling:
1-3/4 cups ricotta cheese, drained
1/4 lb. dried sausage of salami, chopped
2 egg yolks
1/4 cup fresh parsley, minced
Salt and freshly ground black pepper

1. In a large bowl, combine both flours, salt and butter. Mix with a pastry blender or your hands until dough resembles coarse cornmeal. Add egg and milk and continue mixing until dough forms a ball. Wrap dough in plastic wrap, refrigerate until well chilled, at least 20 minutes. (You may mix dough in a food processor with the metal blade.)

2. Mix ricotta, sausage, egg yolks, parsley, add salt and pepper to taste. Refrigerate 15 to 20 minutes.

3. Roll chilled dough out on to lightly floured surface to 1/8" thickness. Cut into circles with 4 inch Tartmaster. Place about 1 tbl. filling in center of each circle. Fold dough over filling. Seal with Tartmaster.

4. Heat oil to 375° F. Fry turnovers until golden brown, about 2 to 3 minutes each. Drain on paper toweling. Serve hot.

Makes 3 dozen turnovers.

Stuffed Pizza

ITALIAN SAUSAGE AND SPINACH PIE

1 lb. hot, Italian sausage, casings removed
1 lb. fresh spinach, stems removed, chopped OR 1 pkg. (10 oz.) frozen chopped
    spinach, thawed, squeezed
      1 cup shredded Mozzarella cheese
      Pizza dough (see Stuffed Pizza dough page 62)
      1 tbl. olive oil
      Freshly ground black pepper

1. Cook sausage in large skillet until well-browned; drain fat. Add spinach. Cook until spinach wilts, about 3 minutes. Cool slightly.

2. Roll out dough on lightly floured surface to a 12 x 10 inch rectangle. Transfer dough to an oiled baking sheet.

3. Spoon sausage mixture evenly over half of the dough lengthwise leaving a 3/4 inch border. Cover with the shredded cheese. Fold dough over filling. Press and seal edges of dough with Krimpkut Sealer.

4. Brush top of dough with olive oil. Sprinkle with pepper to taste. Make several slits in top of dough with knife. Bake in lower third of preheated 400° oven until well-browned, 15 to 20 minutes.

Makes 4 to 6 servings.

PIZZA RUSTICA

PASTRY:
1-1/2 cups whole wheat flour
1/2 cup all-purpose flour
1/4 tsp. salt
6 tbl. butter or margarine
1/4 cup vegetable shortening
4-6 tbl. cold water

Filling:
3 tbl. vegetable oil
2 red peppers, seeded and chopped
2 zucchini, sliced
1/2 cup chopped onion
1 lb. eggplant, pared and cubed
1/2 lb. mushrooms, sliced
1 clove garlic, minced
1/2 tsp. oregano
1/2 tsp. salt
1/4 tsp. pepper
2 tbl. whole wheat flour
1 container (15 oz.) Ricotta cheese
1/2 cup shredded Mozzarella cheese
1/2 cup grated Parmesan cheese
2 eggs, lightly beaten
1/3 cup chopped Italian parsley
1 egg white
1 tbl. water

Pastry:

1. Combine flours and salt. Cut in butter and shortening with pastry blender until mixture resembles coarse meal.

2. Gradually add water, stirring until mixture holds together. Form pastry into a ball.

3. Roll out 3/4 of the pastry on lightly floured surface into a 11 inch circle. Fit pastry into a 9 inch pie plate. Trim pastry, leaving a 1/2 inch overhang.

4. Roll out remaining pastry plus leftover scraps into a 10 inch x 4 inch rectangle, about 1/8 inch thick. Cut lengthwise into 8 strips with Krimpkut Sealer. Place strips on baking sheet; cover with waxed paper.

5. For Filling: Heat oil in large skillet. Saute red pepper, zucchini and onion until tender, about 5 minutes. Add eggplant, mushrooms, garlic, oregano, 1/4 teaspoon of the salt and 1/8 teaspoon of the pepper. Cook, stirring constantly 5 minutes. Cool. Stir in flour.

6. Combine Ricotta, Mozzarella, Parmesan, eggs, parsley, and remaining salt and pepper.

7. Spread half of cheese mixture over bottom of crust. Top with half of vegetables; repeat layers. Place pastry strips across top of pie to form a lattice pattern. Fold edge of pastry over strips; flute edges.

8. Combine egg white and water. Brush over top of pastry. Bake in preheated 350° oven until top is lightly browned. Let stand 10 minutes before cutting.

STUFFED PIZZA

Dough:
1/2 pkg. dry yeast
3/4 cup warm water (105° to 115°)
1/2 tsp. sugar
1/2 tsp. salt
1/4 cup olive oil
1 egg
2 to 2-1/2 cups all-purpose flour

Filling:
1 lb. Italian sausage, cooked and sliced
 Salt and pepper
1 cup Italian plum tomatoes, crushed
1 onion, chopped
1/2 lb. Mozzarella cheese, shredded
1 tbl. minced parsley,
1/4 cup olive oil
1 egg yolk, beaten, for glaze

1. Dissolve yeast in water in medium bowl. Let stand in warm place until bubbly. Add sugar, salt, eggs and enough of the flour to make a smooth dough.

2. Turn dough out on lightly floured surface. Knead until smooth and elastic, about 10 minutes.

3. Stretch or roll out half of dough to fit the bottom of a 14 inch round or square pizza pan at least 2 inches deep.

4. Cover dough with sausage, onion, salt, pepper, cheese, tomatoes, parsley and Parmesan cheese. Sprinkle with oil.

5. Roll out remaining dough and place on top of filling. Seal edges with Krimpkut Sealer.

6. Cover pan with a cloth. Let rise until doubled in size, about 1 hour. Brush top with beaten egg yolk. Bake in preheated 375° oven until top is golden brown, about 45 minutes. Remove from oven and let cool 15 minutes.

Makes 6 servings.

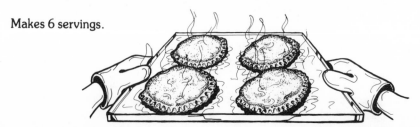

Beef Dinners

BEEFY ONION TARTS

Plain dough (see recipe page 15)
1-1/2 cups thinly sliced onion (3 medium)
1/4 cup chopped green pepper
1/4 cup butter or margarine
2 cups chopped cooked beef
1 cup dairy sour cream
2 tbl. all-purpose flour
3/4 tsp. salt
1/8 tsp. pepper
1 beaten egg
2 tbl. chopped parsley
2 tbl. chopped pimiento

1. Saute onion and green pepper in butter until tender. Stir in beef; remove from heat. Combine sour cream, flour, salt and pepper. Stir in egg, parsley and pimiento. Add to onion-beef mixture; mix well.

2. Roll out pastry on lightly floured board to 1/8 inch thickness. Spoon fillings in mounds on half of pastry about 5 inches apart. Fold over remaining dough. Cut and seal with Tartmaster.

3. Make a few slits in top of each pastry. Place on ungreased baking sheet. Bake in preheated 375⁰ oven until golden 35 to 40 minutes.

CHICKEN PIE

1 chicken, about 3 pounds, cooked
4 leeks, sliced
2 cups chicken broth
1 tsp. sugar
Salt
2 oz. cooked ham
1 tbl. minced parsley
Puff pastry made with 1-1/2 cups flour (reference page 13)
1 egg, beaten
1/4 cup heavy cream

1. Place leeks and broth in saucepan. Heat to boiling; simmer 15 to 20 minutes.

2. Cut cooked chicken into bite size pieces. Arrange in deep pie dish. Add leeks and stock. Sprinkle with sugar and dash of salt. Place thin slices of ham over top.

3. Roll out pastry to 1 inch larger than pie dish. Cover dish with pastry and trim and seal edges with Krimpkut Sealer. Cut a cross in center and brush with beaten egg.

4. Place pie in preheated 350⁰ oven and bake for 45 minutes.
   Heat cream in pan and pour through cross in center.

CORNISH PASTIES

Pastry:
4 cups all-purpose flour
1/4 tsp. salt
1-1/2 cups lard or vegetable shortening (3/4 lb.) chilled and cut into 1/4"
pieces
8 to 10 tbl. ice water

Filling:
2 cups lean boneless beef or any leftover meat, chopped
2 tbl. butter
1 cup cooked white or yellow turnips, coarsely chopped
1 cup coarsely chopped onions
2 cups diced, cooked potatoes
1-1/2 tsp. salt
1 tsp. freshly ground black pepper
1 egg, lightly beaten with 1 tsp. water

1. In large bowl, combine flour, salt and lard. Working quickly, cut in lard with pastry blender or your fingertips until it resembles cornmeal. Pour in 8 tablespoons ice water. Stir and gather the dough into a ball. If dough crumbles, add up to 2 more tablespoons water, 1 teaspoon at a time, until dough adheres. Form into a flattened ball and wrap in waxed paper. Refrigerate at least 1 hour.

2. Cut dough into 4 pieces. Roll out each piece on a lightly floured surface to 1/4 inch thickness. With Krimpkut Sealer, cut the dough into 6 to 8 inch rounds, using a small plate or pot lid as a guide. Gather the scraps together into a ball, roll out again and cut.

3. If the meat has been previously cooked, saute in butter until warm. If raw, saute meat until it loses its red color.

4. Combine meat, turnips, onions, potatoes, salt and pepper. Place about 1/4 cup of the mixture in the center of each pastry round. Moisten the edges of the rounds with a pastry brush dipped in cold water, then fold in half to enclose filling completely. Press seams together and crimp with Krimpkut Sealer.

5. Place pasties on a lightly greased baking sheet. Cut two slits about 1 inch long in the top of each. Brush lightly with egg. Bake in preheated 400° oven for 15 minutes. Reduce temperature to 350°. Continue baking for about 30 minutes or until golden.

FILLET STEAK WASHINGTON

2 lbs. beef tenderloin cut into 4 steaks
4 tbl. clarified butter
Salt
Freshly ground pepper
4 large mushrooms
1 lb. puff pastry (Reference page 13) or Frozen Puff Pastry
1 tsp. lemon juice
Cayenne pepper
1 egg, lightly beaten
Vegetable oil for frying

1. Season steaks with salt and pepper. Heat butter until hot in skillet. Sear steaks on both sides and around edges. (4 minutes for well done on each side 2 minutes for rare). Remove steaks from skillet; cool.

2. Cook mushrooms in skillet with lemon juice, and cayenne pepper until barely tender. Remove from skillet. Place one mushroom on top of cooled steaks.

3. Roll out puff pastry on lightly floured surface to 1/8 inch thickness. Cut out 4 circles of pastry 1/2 inch larger than size of steaks. Cut out 4 more circles about 1-1/2 inches larger than steaks.

4. Brush small rounds of pastry with egg. Top with steak and mushroom. Brush larger pastry round with egg. Place over steak. Seal edges of pastry with Krimpkut Sealer.

5. Cover and refrigerate overnight. Remove from refrigerator 30 minutes before cooking.

6. Heat oil to 375°. Fry pastries until golden, about 7 minutes. Drain on paper toweling. Serve with small minted potatoes.

Makes 4 servings.

GREEK FREIGHTER MEAT PIE
Puff Pastry or Plan Dough

2 tbl. butter or margarine
2 onion, chopped
2 cups cooked meat chopped; beef, lamb, pork or veal OR 1 lb. ground beef, lamb, pork or veal
1 cup rice OR 1 cup diced potatoes
1 tsp. dried mint leaves
1 tsp. marjoram
1/2 cup minced parsley
1 tsp. salt
1 cup feta cheese
1 egg, lightly beaten
1/2 cup pine nuts or walnuts
pepper to taste

1. Saute onions in butter until tender. If using raw meat and potatoes, brown meat 5 minutes. Add 1 cup hot water for potatoes and 2 cups water if using rice.

2. Add mint, marjoram, parsley and salt. Simmer, covered until potatoes or rice are tender. Remove from heat.

3. Stir in cheese, egg and nuts. Cool filling before using.

4. Roll out pastry to 1 inch larger than pie dish. Cover pie dish with pastry.

5. Add Filling.

6. Roll out second sheet of pastry. Place on top and trim and seal edges with Krimpkut Sealer. Cut vents in top.

7. Place pie in preheated 350° oven and bake until golden, about 30 minutes.

LATTICED LOBSTER TART

2 tbl. unsalted butter
1 1-lb. lobster, boiled, shell discarded, meat finely chopped or 1/2 lb. cooked
    shelled shrimp
Ground red pepper
2 tbl. dry sherry
1 tbl. whole wheat flour
1/3 cup sour cream
1 tbl. chopped fresh dill or 1 tsp. dried dillweed
1/2 lb. puff pastry (reference page 13) or frozen puff pastry
1 egg, beaten

1. Melt butter in medium skillet over low heat. Add lobster and sprinkle with ground red pepper. Cook until warmed through, about 1 to 2 minutes. Remove from heat. Warm sherry in small saucepan over medium-high heat. Remove from heat, ignite and pour over lobster.

2. Sprinkle lobster with flour. Stir in sour cream and dill. Transfer mixture to bowl and let cool; refrigerate.

3. Roll dough out on lightly floured surface into large rectangle to thickness of about 1/8 inch. Cut into 2 equal rectangles. Transfer 1 rectangle to dampened baking sheet and set aside. Fold remaining rectangle in half lengthwise.

4. Cut 1/2 inch strips with Krimpkut Sealer long folded side to within 1/2 inch of open edge. Brush edges of uncut pastry rectangle with water.

5. Spread lobster mixture down center. Unfold cut rectangle and set over lobster mixture aligning with bottom edges. Seal with Krimpkut Sealer. Chill tart in refrigerator at least 30 minutes.

6. Brush chilled tart with beaten egg. Bake in preheated 400° oven until golden brown, about 30 minutes.

MEAT DUMPLINGS

Dough:
2 cups all-purpose flour
1/2 cup hot water

1. Mix flour and enough water to make a soft dough. Cover with a damp cloth and let stand at least 20 minutes.

2. Knead dough again and form into a long sausage 1-1/2 inches in diameter. Cut into 1/3 inch pieces.

3. Flatten pieces with palm of hand. Roll into thin circles about 4 inches in diameter.

Filling:
8 oz. Chinese cabbage or celery, finely chopped
1 leek, chopped
8 oz. ground pork
1 tsp. grated ginger
1/2 tsp. salt
1 tbl. white table wine
3 tbl. sesame oil
Dash of pepper
Dash of monosodium glutamate
Soy Sauce
Vinegar

1. Combine cabbage, leek, ginger, salt, wine, oil, pepper and monosodium glutamate.

2. Place about 1 teaspoon of filling in the center of each circle. Fold into half-moon shapes.

3. Seal edges with Krimpkut Sealer or Tartmaster.

4. To cook, drop dumplings in boiling water, one by one. Cook until tender. Serve with small dishes of soy sauce and vinegar mixed to taste.

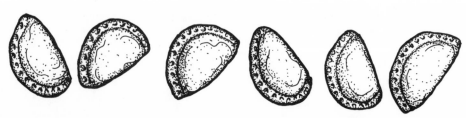

MEAT FILLED RAVIOLI

Ravioli Dough:
2 cups all-purpose flour, sifted
3 egg yolks
Pinch of Salt

1. Combine all ingredients for meat filling. Set aside

2. Mound flour on board. Make a well in the center. Place egg yolks, pinch of salt, and a little lukewarm water in well. Beat egg mixture in well with a fork until smooth. Gradually work in flour with egg mixture until firm, but not dry dough.

3. Knead dough on floured board until smooth. Shape into ball. Brush lightly with olive oil. Cover and let rest 20 minutes. Roll dough on floured board until very thin. Cut dough into 2 equal parts.

4. Place mixture by teaspoonful in nicely spaced rows about 2 inches apart on one of the sheets. Cover with remaining sheet of dough. Using Krimpkut Sealer, cut ravioli in uniform sizes by running the wheel between the mounds.

5. Drop the ravioli into boiling chicken broth or lightly salted water. Cook until tender, 5 to 10 minutes. Drain, serve with tomato sauce and grated cheese.

Meat Filling:
2 cups cooked ground beef
1/2 cup cooked chopped spinach, drained well
1/2 cup grated Parmesan cheese
1/4 cup minced parsley
1/2 cup dry bread crumbs
1/2 cup minced Genoa salami
3 eggs
Salt and pepper to taste

Variations: 3 slices minced Prosciutto ham and a pinch of nutmeg added to the meat filling is a nice flavor combination for "Angelotti".

One pound fresh Ricotta cheese can be used in place of meat or poultry.

Two cups cooked, chopped white poultry meat or 2 cups cooked ground pork may be used instead of, or in conjunction with, the ground beef.

NATCHITOCHES MEAT PIES

Pastry:
2 cups self-rising flour
1/2 cup vegetable shortening
2 eggs, lightly beaten
1/3 cup milk

Filling:
1 lb. ground pork
8 oz. ground beef
1/2 cup chopped white onions
1/2 cup chopped green onions
1 clove garlic, miniced
1/8 tsp. freshly ground black pepper
1/8 tsp. cayenne pepper
1 tsp. salt
1/4 cup all-purpose flour
2 tbl. water
2 tbl. minced parsley
Vegetable oil for frying

1. Sift 2 cups flour into large mixing bowl. Cut shortening into flour until it resembles coarse cornmeal.

2. Stir in eggs and milk to make a soft dough. Cover and refrigerate 1 to 2 hours.

3. To make filling, saute pork, beef, onions, garlic, pepper and salt in large saucepan until meat loses its pink color, about 10 minutes. Add 1/4 cup flour and cook, stirring until mixture thickens, about 3 minutes.

4. Add water and parsley. Simmer, stirring occasionally, 5 minutes. Drain excess fat from mixture. Cool mixture. Refrigerate 1 hour.

5. Roll out 1/4 of the pastry (keep remainder refrigerated) on lightly floured surface as thin as possible. Cut into circles using 3 inch or 4 inch Tartmaster.

6. Place about 1-1/2 teaspoons for small circles and level tablespoon for large circles on one half of each pastry. Fold tops of pastry over filling. Seal with Tartmaster.

7. Pierce tops of pastry twice. Heat oil to 365° to 375°. Fry pies, a few at a time, turning once or twice about 4 minutes or until golden. Drain on paper toweling. Serve hot.

OLD ENGLISH PORK PIE

1 lb. ground lean pork
1/8 tsp. sage
1 egg, lightly beaten
1 tsp. salt
1/2 tsp. freshly ground pepper
1/2 cup all-purpose flour
1 lb. lean pork, cut into 1/2 inch strips
8 slices bacon, diced
1 cup Spanish onion, chopped
2 tbl. butter
1/2 tsp. thyme
1/4 tsp. cinnamon
2 tbl. parsley, finely chopped
1-1/4 cups red wine
1-1/4 cups beef broth
1/2 recipe Basic Puff Pastry dough (see recipe page 13)

1. Combine the ground pork, sage, egg, 1/2 teaspoon of the salt and 1/4 teaspoon of the pepper in a bowl. Shape into 1 inch balls. Combine the flour, remaining 1/2 teaspoon of salt and 1/4 teaspoon of pepper. Dredge the balls with the flour mixture.

2. Cut the pork into 1/2 inch strips; dredge with the remaining flour mixture. Fry the bacon until crisp. Remove bacon with a slotted spoon and drain on paper toweling. Brown the pork balls, then the pork strips in the bacon drippings. Remove with a slotted spoon and place on paper toweling to drain.

3. Saute the onion in the butter until lightly browned. Combine the pork strips, onion, thyme, cinnamon, parsley, wine and broth in a deep 9 inch casserole. Arrange the pork balls over the top; cover.

4. Bake in a preheated 350° oven for 1 hour or until the pork is fork tender, adding more broth if needed. Remove from the oven and cool thoroughly.

5. Roll out the pastry on a lightly floured surface to 1/8 inch thickness. Trim to fit the top of the casserole. Place pastry on the cold casserole. Brush with egg glaze. Cut 1/2 inch strips of the remaining pastry with the Krimpkut Sealer. Twist strips, then arrange twists around the slightly moistened edge and center. Brush the trim with the glaze.

6. Bake in a preheated 375° oven for 25 minutes or until browned. Serve immediately. This is an excellent do-ahead dish as the pie filling is cooked and cooled before the pastry topping is added and baked again.

Makes 6 to 8 servings.

PILAF TURNOVERS

3/4 cup water
1/2 tsp. salt
1/2 cup quick-cooking brown rice
3 cups sliced fresh mushrooms
3 tbl. butter or margarine
1 3 oz. pkg. cream cheese with chives, cut up
1 medium carrot, shredded
1/4 cup chopped almonds, toasted
2 tbl. milk
1/2 tsp. dried basil
2 frozen pie shells
1 egg white mixed with 1 tbl. water
Parsley sprigs

1. In saucepan, bring 3/4 cup water and the salt to boiling; add rice. Reduce heat; cover and simmer 15 minutes or till water is absorbed.

2. Meanwhile, cook mushrooms in butter or margarine until tender. Stir cooked rice and cream cheese into mushrooms until cheese is melted. Stir in carrot, almonds, milk, and basil. Set aside.

3. Invert frozen pastry shells onto waxed paper; remove pie tins. Let pastry thaw for 10 to 15 minutes or until flattened. (If necessary, pat thawed pastry with hands to flatten.) Spread half of the filling over half of each pastry round to about 1/2 inch from edge; fold dough over filling to form a half-moon shape. Seal with Krimpkut Sealer. Brush turnovers with egg-white mixture. Pierce crusts with fork. Using large spatula, transfer turnovers to an ungreased baking sheet. Bake in preheated 375° oven until golden, 25 to 30 minutes. If necessary, cover edges of pastry with foil the last 15 minutes of baking to prevent overbrowning. Transfer turnovers to serving platter; garnish with parsley.

Makes 6 servings.

PORK AND SWEET POTATO PIE

2 medium sweet potatoes
1 lb. boneless pork, cut into 1/2 inch cubes
2 tbl. vegetable oil
1/2 cup chopped onion
1/2 cup chopped green pepper
2 tbl. all-purpose flour
1 tsp. instant chicken bouillon granules
1 tsp. ground sage
1/4 tsp. salt
1/8 tsp. pepper
1 cup water
1 pkg. (10 oz.) frozen, chopped broccoli, thawed

Cornmeal Pastry:
1-3/4 cups all-purpose flour
1/2 cup cornmeal
1 tsp. salt
3/4 cup shortening
5 to 7 tbl. water

1. Cook sweet potatoes in boiling, salted water for 25 minutes or until just tender. Drain, peel, and slice potatoes; set aside.

2. Brown pork cubes, half at a time, in hot oil in skillet over high heat; remove meat from skillet. Reserve about 2 tablespoons drippings in skillet, adding more cooking oil of necessary. Cook onion and green pepper in reserved drippings until tender.

3. Stir in flour, bouillon granules, sage, salt and pepper. Stir in water. Cook and stir until thickened and bubbly. Stir in cooked pork, potatoes and thawed broccoli. Heat through; keep warm.

4. For pastry: place flour, cornmeal and salt in mixing bowl. Cut in shortening with pastry blender until mixture resembles coarse meal. Add water, 1 tablespoon at a time and mix until dough forms a ball.

5. Roll out 2/3 of pastry on lightly floured surface to a rectangle 15 x 11 inches. Fit dough into bottom and up sides of 12 x 7-1/2 inch baking dish. Trim pastry to within 1/2 inch of dish.

6. Spoon pork mixture into crust. Roll out remaining pastry to 12 x 6 inch rectangle. Using Krimpkut Sealer, cut dough into 1 inch strips.

7. Place dough strips atop filling in parallel fashion about 1 inch apart. Trim pastry strips even with bottom crust. Fold bottom pastry over lattice strips to build up the edge.

8. Bake pie in preheated 375° oven 40 minutes or until golden. Cut into square to serve.

Makes 6 servings.

PRIDDY OGGY

Cheese Pastry:
About 1-3/4 cups all-purpose flour, sifted
Pinch of salt
1/4 cup butter, cut into pieces
1/4 cup lard, cut into pieces
1/2 cup grated sharp cheddar cheese
6 tbl. water

Meat Filling:
1/4 lb. pork tenderloin
3 thin slices smoked pork loin
1/4 cup shredded sharp cheddar cheese
Pinch dried sage
Pinch dried thyme
Freshly ground salt and pepper

1. Place flour and salt in bowl. Make a well in the center. Cut in butter and lard with pastry blender until mixture resembles coarse meal.

2. Add cheese. Stir in enough water to form a dough. Knead lightly on floured surface. Cover and refrigerate 30 minutes.

3. Roll out pastry on lightly floured surface into an 8 inch circle.

4. Butterfly pork tenderloin by cutting almost in half. Pound meat to thin out.

5. Place pastry round on greased baking sheet. Lay flattened pork in center of pastry. Cover with 2 slices of smoked pork loin and cheddar cheese. Lay third slice of pork loin on top.

6. Sprinkle with crumbled sage leaf, thyme, salt and pepper. Brush edges of pastry with water. Enclose filling by bringing edges to top. Seal with Krimpkut Sealer. Bake in preheated 375° oven about 1 hour.

SCALLOPS WITH ROQUEFORT IN PASTRY

3/4 lb. puff pastry (see recipe page 13)
1 egg beaten with 1 tbl. milk
3/4 lb. bay scallops
6 oz. (1-1/2 sticks) unsalted butter, at room temperature
4 oz. Roquefort cheese, crumbled (about 1/2 cup) at room temperature
1-1/2 tbl. minced parsley
1 tbl. flour
Freshly ground white pepper to taste
1/2 cup heavy cream

1. Roll out pastry on a lightly floured board into a rectangle 12 x 15 inches. Trim all edges with Krimpkut Sealer, cutting straight down through the dough.

2. Sprinkle a baking sheet with cold water. Transfer pastry to sheet, placing it upside down. Refrigerate 2 hours.

3. Brush pastry with egg mixture, taking care not to let it run over edge. Bake in a preheated 425° oven until puffed and golden, 15 to 17 minutes. Turn off oven. leave pastry in oven with door closed 8 minutes longer.

4. Meanwhile, prepare filling: heat 2 cups water to boiling. Add scallops; blanch 15 seconds. Drain well; set aside.

5. Process butter, Roquefort, parsley, flour and pepper in food processor with metal blade using on/off motion 4 times. Scrape down bowl.

6. Heat cream in saucepan to simmer. Remove from heat. Add Roquefort mixture; whisk until smooth.

7. Return to simmer. Stir in scallops and correct seasoning. Simmer 2 minutes.

8. Split baked pastry horizontally. Spoon filling over bottom half. Replace top lightly press down. Cut pastry crosswise into 4 strips.

Makes 4 servings.

Favorite Dinner Fillings

The following fillings can be used with either the puff pastry or plain dough recipe, as well as with a frozen, prepared puff pastry. Prepare the pastry or dough and the filling as directed. Shape the pastry or dough of your choice, fill and seal. Use the Tartmaster for making individual round or half moon tarts. Or, use the Krimpkut Sealer for sealing turnovers, squares, or large pie-shaped or rectangular entrees that can be sliced when served. For individually portioned tarts, bake the puff pastry or plain dough at 375⁰ for approximately 10 minutes until lightly browned. Bake at 350⁰ for 25-30 minutes for large entrees.

Insert Basic Puff Pastry Recipe

Insert Plain Dough Recipe

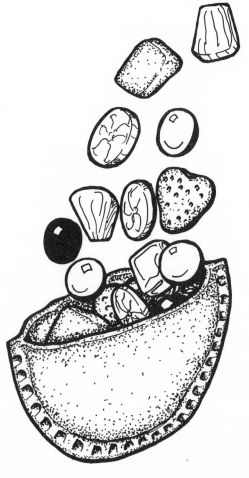

CRETAN CHICKEN FILLING

4 cups cooked, chopped chicken
5 green onions, chopped
2 cups milk
1 tbl. butter
2 eggs, beaten
1 tsp. salt
3 tbl. cornstarch
Freshly ground pepper to taste

1. Combine cornstarch and 1/2 cup of the milk. Heat remaining milk to boiling. Stir in cornstarch mixture, salt and butter.

2. Heat to boiling, stirring constantly until thickened. Remove from heat. Stir in chicken, onions and eggs.

CURRIED CHICKEN FILLING

4 tsp. cornstarch
3/4 tsp. salt
1 boneless chicken breast (about 6 oz.), skinned, coarsely chopped
2 tbl. chicken broth
2 tbl. vegetable oil
1 tbl. dry sherry
1/2 cup chopped onion
1-1/2 tsp. curry powder
1 tsp. sugar
2 tbl. chopped green onion, green part only

1. In a 2-quart mixing bowl stir together 1 tsp. of the cornstarch with 1/4 tsp. salt. Add the chopped chicken breast and stir well. Cover with plastic wrap and set aside at room temperature for 30 minutes.

2. Stir together the remaining 3 tsp. cornstarch with the chicken broth; set aside.

3. In a medium skillet, heat 1 tbl. of the oil over moderate heat. Add the chicken and cook, stirring constantly, until the pieces have separated, about 1 minute. Sprinkle with sherry. Transfer to a side dish with a slotted spoon.

4. Heat the remaining oil in the skillet over moderate heat. Add the onion and cook, stirring constantly, until translucent, about 1 minute. Add the curry powder and stir for 30 seconds. Stir in the sugar, the remaining 1/2 tsp. salt and the reserved chicken.

5. Add the reserved cornstarch and broth mixture and stir until the sauce thickens and coats the chicken. Stir in the green onion. Transfer to a side dish to cool to room temperature. Filling will keep, covered, for a week in the refrigerator or it may be frozen for up to 3 months.

HAM FILLING

1 cup finely chopped country ham
1 heaping tbl. Dijon-style mustard
1 tbl. chutney, minced
1 tsp. vinegar
2 green onions, minced
Sour cream and mayonnaise

1. Combine ham, mustard, chutney, vinegar and onions. Add enough sour cream and mayonnaise to bind mixture. Use as a filling for fried bread cases.

MEAT SAUCE

1 onion, chopped
2 tbl. butter
1 carrot, chopped
1 small stalk celery, chopped
1 cup mushrooms, sliced
1 tbl. minced parsley
8 ounces ground beef
1 tbl. flour
2 tsp. tomato paste
6 tbl. white wine
1/4 cup beef broth
salt and pepper

1. Saute onion in butter in saucepan until tender. Add remaining vegetables and parsley. Cook until lightly browned.

2. Add beef, cook until brown. Stir in flour. Add tomato paste, wine and broth. Season with salt and pepper. Simmer uncovered 30 to 40 minutes.

MEAT AND VEGETABLE FILLING

6 oz. fresh mushrooms
2 tbl. vegetable oil
8 oz. lean pork, cut into 2 inch cubes
1-1/2 tsp. soy sauce
1-1/2 tsp. dry sherry
1 tsp. cornstarch
1 can (5 oz.) bamboo shoots, drained
1 pkg. (10 oz.) frozen chopped kale or chopped collard greens, thawed and squeezed very dry
1/2 tsp. salt
1/2 tsp. sugar
Pinch of freshly ground white pepper

1. Coarsely chop mushrooms in food processor fitted with metal blade using on/off motion.

2. Heat 1 tbl. of the oil in a medium skillet over moderate heat. Add the mushrooms and cook, stirring, until their moisture has been released and evaporated, about 5 minutes. Transfer to a side dish and set aside.

3. Using metal blade coarsely chop the pork, using on/off motion. Transfer to a 2-quart mixing bowl. Stir in soy sauce, sherry and cornstarch. Set aside.

4. Using metal blade, coarsely chop bamboo shoots, using on/off motion.

5. Heat the remaining tablespoon of oil in a wok or medium skillet over moderately high heat. Add pork mixture and cook, stirring constantly, just until the pork loses its pink color. Add bamboo shoots and stir for 1 minute. Add the kale and reserved mushrooms and mix well.

6. Stir in the salt, sugar and pepper. Cool to room temperature. The filling will keep, covered for a week in the refrigerator or it may be frozen for up to 3 months.

Variation:

Substitute 8 ounces seasoned pressed bean curd for the pork and omit the cornstarch.

PICADILLO, YUCATAN STYLE

1 lb. ground beef
2 tbl. vegetable oil
1 medium onion, finely chopped
1 clove garlic, minced
1 medium tomato, peeled, seeded, chopped
1 tbl. capers, minced
15 olives, minced
2 hard-cooked eggs, chopped
salt and pepper to taste

1. Saute beef until browned. Drain fat and remove from pan.

2. Heat oil in skillet. Add remaining ingredients except eggs. Cook 3 to 4 minutes. Add drained meat and eggs.

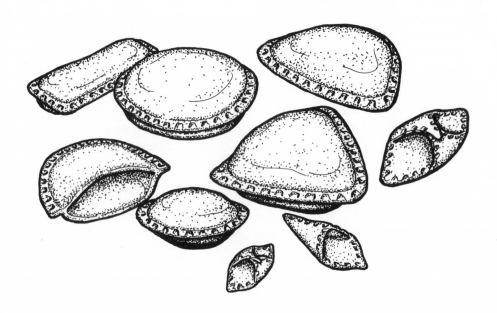

RATATOUILLE FILLING

1 medium eggplant
1/3 cup olive oil
2 medium onions, finely chopped
1 large red sweet pepper, cut into strips
3 small zucchini, thinly sliced
2 small garlic cloves, pressed
2 tsp. minced parsley
4 medium tomatoes, peeled and chopped
1-1/2 tsp. salt
1/4 tsp. freshly ground pepper
1 tsp. sugar

1. Trim the stem from the eggplant but do not peel. Cut into 1/2 inch slices, then cut into cubes. Place the eggplant slices in a bowl with salted water to cover. Weight the eggplant down with a plate. Let soak for at least 15 minutes.

2. Heat oil in Dutch oven. Add onions, pepper and zucchini. Cover and cook 4 minutes, stirring occasionally. Add garlic and parsley.

3. Drain eggplant. Add to onion mixture. Cover and cook 5 minutes. Add tomatoes, salt, pepper and sugar. Cover and cook until eggplant is tender about 10 minutes longer.

ROAST PORK FILLING

2 tbl. cornstarch
2 tbl. water
1 tbl. vegetable oil
1 cup chopped onion
2 cups chopped roast pork
2 tbl. soy sauce
1 tbl. sugar
Pinch of salt
Pinch of freshly ground white pepper
1/4 cup chopped green onions

1. Mix cornstarch and 2 tbl. water; set aside.

2. Heat oil in wok or skillet over moderate heat. Add onion and cook until tender, about 2 minutes.

3. Stir in pork, remaining 2 tbl. water, the soy sauce, sugar, salt and pepper. Stir in cornstarch mixture and green onions. Cook until mixture has thickened.

4. Remove from heat. Set aside to cool. Cover and refrigerate up to 1 week or freeze up to 3 months.

Desserts

ALMOND TRIANGLES

1/2 cup butter
1 cup sugar
6 tbl. heavy cream
3 eggs
1/2 tsp. salt
2 cups all-purpose flour
Chopped almonds

1. Cream butter and sugar until light and fluffy. Beat in cream and 2 of the eggs. Add flour and salt; mix well. Wrap in plastic wrap. Refrigerate overnight.

2. Roll out dough on lightly floured surface to 1/4 inch thickness. Cut into triangles with Krimpkut Sealer.

3. Beat remaining egg. Brush over top surfaces of the triangles. Sprinkle with almonds. Place on greased baking sheets. Bake in preheated 375° oven until golden, 8 to 10 minutes.

Makes 3 to 4 dozen cookies.

APPLE DUMPLINGS

Pastry Dough:
2 cups sifted flour
1 tsp. salt
1/2 cup shortening
3/4 cup milk, approximately
2 tsp. baking powder

Filling:
6 small apples, pared and cored
1/2 cup sugar
1/4 tsp. cinnamon
2 tbl. butter or margarine

Sauce Mixture:
1/2 cup firmly packed brown sugar
1/3 cup butter or margarine
Pinch of nutmeg
Pinch of cinnamon
1-1/3 cups hot water

1. Place flour, baking powder and salt in mixing bowl. Cut in shortening with pastry blender until mixture resembles coarse cornmeal. Stir in milk to make a soft dough.

2. Turn out on lightly floured surface. Knead until smooth. Roll out to 1/8 inch thickness. Cut into squares with Krimpkut Sealer. Cut squares large enough to hold a whole small apple. Combine sugar and cinnamon. Fill the core of the apple with a little of this mixture. Divide butter among apples.

3. Moisten edges of dough with water. Bring edges of dough up over apple. Seal with Krimpkut Sealer. Place dumplings in greased baking pan, making sure they do not touch each other. Pierce pastry with fork.

4. For sauce, combine brown sugar, nutmeg, cinnamon, butter and hot water. Heat until sugar dissolves. Pour sauce mixture over dumplings.

5. Bake in preheated 450° oven for 15 minutes. Decrease temperature to 350° and bake 25 minutes longer or until apples are tender. Serve warm with pan sauces and milk or cream.

APRICOT FRIED PIES

1-1/3 cups all-purpose flour
2 tsp. baking powder
1 tsp. salt
6 tbl. shortening
1 egg, slightly beaten
About 1/2 cup milk
Vegetable oil or shortening for frying

Apricot Filling:
2 cups cooked, dried apricots
3/4 cup sugar
1/4 tsp. cinnamon
Combine all ingredients for filling.

1. Sift flour, baking powder and salt into mixing bowl. Cut in shortening until small particles are formed. Place egg in measuring cup. Add enough milk to measure 2/3 cup. Add to dry ingredients. Mix until dough has formed.

2. Roll out dough on lightly floured board to 1/8 inch thickness. Place filling by tablespoons over 1/2 of dough allowing enough room between for the cutter. Brush remaining half of dough with water. Place dough over filling pressing gently around each mount. Dip Tartmaster in flour. Place over filling and press knob down firmly.

3. Heat oil to 325⁰. Fry pies until golden on each side. Drain on paper toweling. Serve warm sprinkled with powdered sugar. The fried pies can be made ahead of time and reheated.

BANBURY TURNOVERS

1/4 cup chopped walnuts
1/4 cup chopped figs
1/2 cup seedless raisins
1/4 cup firmly packed brown sugar
1 tbl. flour
2 tbl. lemon juice
1 tbl. grated lemon rind
Pie pastry (reference page 15)

1. Combine walnuts, raisins, figs, sugar, flour, lemon juice and rind.

2. Roll out pastry on lightly floured surface to 1/8 inch thickness. Cut into 4 inch squares with Krimpkut Sealer.

3. Place 1 tablespoon fruit mixture in center of each square. Moisten edges with water. Fold dough over to form a triangle. Seal with Krimpkut Sealer. Make slits in top of turnovers. Bake in preheated 450° oven until golden, about 15 minutes.

BERRY POCKETS

1 to 1-1/4 cups biscuit mix
2 tbl. sugar
1/3 cup heavy cream
1 cup fresh berries
2 tsp. granulated sugar
1/4 tsp. cinnamon
1/4 tsp. grated lemon rind
Heavy cream
1 tsp. granulated sugar

1. Combine biscuit mix and sugar. Stir in 1/3 cup cream or enough to make a fairly stiff dough. Knead dough on lightly floured board about 10 times.

2. Roll dough on lightly floured surface into a 12 inch square. Cut into 9 squares with Krimpkut Sealer.

3. Combine berries, 2 teaspoons sugar, cinnamon and lemon rind. Place a spoonful of berry mixture on one side of each square. Fold one corner of square over fruit making a triangle. Seal edges with Krimpkut Sealer.

4. Place on greased baking sheet. Cut 2 small slits in top of each pastry. Brush tops with cream. Sprinkle with remaining 1 teaspoon sugar.

5. Bake in preheated 425° oven until golden, about 12 minutes. Serve hot.

Makes 9 pockets.

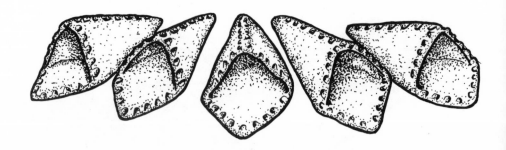

BISMARKS
(Filled Doughnuts)

7 oz. bakers cheese
6 tbl. milk
1 egg
1/2 cup sugar
1 tsp. vanilla
1-1/2 cups all-purpose flour
1-1/2 tsp. baking powder
Fruit jelly or preserves, apricot or prune filling
Lightly beaten egg
Vegetable oil

1. Cream bakers cheese, milk, egg, sugar and vanilla. Stir in flour and baking powder. Place dough on lightly floured board. Knead until smooth.

2. Roll out half of dough to thickness of 1/4 inch. Drop mounds of jelly onto dough. Brush dough with beaten egg. Roll out remaining dough. Place over top. Cut with 3" Tartmaster.

3. Heat vegetable oil in deep fat fryer or electric skillet to 360° F. Place bismarks into fat. Fry until golden brown. Drain on paper toweling.

BUGNES

1 pkg. yeast
1 cup warm water (105° to 115°)
5 cups all-purpose flour
1/2 tsp. salt
3 tbl. sugar
1/2 cup butter, softened
6 eggs
2 tbl. brandy
2 cup confectioners' sugar
2 tsp. nutmeg
2 tsp. cinnamon

1. Dissolve yeast in 1 cup of water. Combine 1 cup of flour and the yeast mixture to form a starter. Shape the starter into a ball and cut a cross on top with scissors. Place the starter in a 2 quart bowl of warm water. The starter will sink to the bottom. Let stand for about 5 to 7 minutes or until the ball rises to the top of the water.

2. While the starter is standing, prepare the dough. Sift the remaining 4 cups of flour, the salt and sugar together into a large bowl. Make a well in the center. Beat the butter until creamy and place in the well. Add the eggs, one at a time, beating well after each addition. Add the brandy and mix the dough well. Shape into a ball on a heavily floured surface and knead until smooth and elastic.

3. Lift the starter from the bowl of water with your hands and let the excess water drip off. Place the starter on a piece of waxed paper. Flatten the dough with your hands. Place the starter on the dough. Work the 2 mixtures together with the pastry scrapers until the 2 mixtures hold together. Knead on a heavily floured board only until well combined. The dough will be sticky.

4. Place the dough in a greased bowl and cover with a towel. Let rise in a warm place for about 1 hour and 30 minutes or until doubled in bulk.

5. Punch down the dough. Roll out dough on heavily floured surface to 1/16 inch thickness. Cut with 3 inch or 4 inch Tartmaster. Place the pieces on a lightly floured baking sheet and let rise for about 30 minutes or until doubled in bulk.

6. Fry in oil heated to 375° until lightly browned on each side. Drain on paper toweling. Combine confectioners' sugar and spices in a paper bag. Toss fried Bugnes, shaking to coat well.

how to fold bugnes

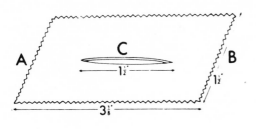

1 Cut a rectangular cardboard pattern 3 1/8 inches long and 1 1/2 inches wide. Using the pattern cut the dough into rectangles with a pastry wheel. Make a 1 1/2-inch lengthwise slit through the center with the pastry wheel.

2 Push A under and completely up through C.

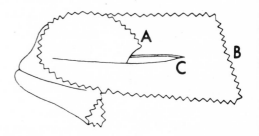

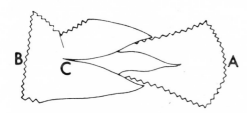

3 The strips should be shaped as shown and flattened slightly.

BUNUELOS

2 cups all-purpose flour
2 tsp. sugar
1/2 tsp. baking powder
1/4 tsp. salt
1 egg
1/3 cup milk
2 tbl. melted butter
Vegetable oil or shortening for frying
Cinnamon
Sugar

1. In medium bowl, combine flour, sugar, baking powder and salt. Add eggs, milk and melted butter. Mix to form a soft dough. On lightly floured board knead about 2 minutes or until smooth. Cover and let stand 30 minutes.

2. Roll out dough on lightly floured surface to 1/8 inch thickness. Cut into rounds with 3 inch Tartmaster

3. Heat oil to 375°. Fry 1 or 2 at a time, until golden and puffy, about 1-1/2 minutes. Drain on paper toweling. Serve warm sprinkled with cinnamon and sugar.

Makes about 2 dozen.

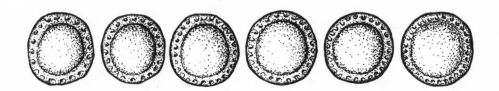

CHEESE STRUDEL

1 pkg. (17-1/4 oz.) puff pastry
1/2 lb. bakers cheese
2 egg yolks
1/3 cup sugar
1 cup ground blanched almonds
1 tbl. all-purpose flour
1/2 cup dark seedless raisins
1 tsp. grated lemon rind
1 egg beaten with 1 tsp. water

1. Thaw pastry sheets 20 minutes. Mix cheese, egg yolks, sugar, almonds, flour, raisins and lemon rind.

2. Cut each pastry sheet in half crosswise. Place 2 of the rectangles on a baking sheet. Spread evenly with cheese mixture to within 3/4 inch of the edges.

3 Brush edges with egg mixture. Cut a 3/4 inch hole in the center of the remaining 2 pastry rectangles. Place on top of cheese filling. Seal with Krimpkut Sealer.

4. Brush tops of pastry with egg mixture. Bake in preheated 425° oven for 35 to 40 minutes or until puffed and golden. Remove to wire rack. Serve warm or cool.

Makes 12 servings.

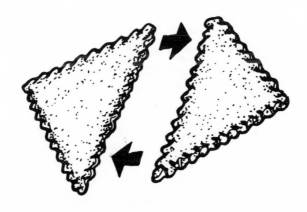

CREAM CHEESE KOLACKY

1 pkg. (8 oz.) cream cheese
1 cup unsalted butter
2 egg yolks
1/3 cup sugar
1-3/4 cups all-purpose flour
2 tsp. baking powder
1/4 tsp. salt
2 cans (12 oz. each) fruit filling
Confectioners' sugar

1. Cream together the cheese and butter. Add egg yolk and mix well. Add sugar and sifted dry ingredients. Blend well. Roll out dough on lightly floured surface to 1/4 inch thickness. Cut into rounds with 3 inch Tartmaster. Top with desired filling.

2. Place on ungreased baking sheets. Bake in preheated 375⁰ oven for 10 to 12 minutes. When cool, sprinkle with confectioners' sugar.

Cheese Topping: (if making cheese-filled kolacky)
2 pkgs. (3 oz. each) cream cheese
3/4 cup sugar
1 tsp. lemon juice
1/2 tsp. vanilla
1 egg yolk

1. Beat together all ingredients. Top kolacky.

CURACAO MARMALADE PIE

Pastry for 2-crust pie (reference page 15)

2 oranges
Juice of 1/2 lemon
1/2 cup water
1-1/4 cups sugar
2-1/2 tbl. cornstarch
1/4 cup butter, softened
3 eggs (reserve 1 tsp. egg to brush top crust)
1 tsp. water (mix with 1 tsp. egg)
2 tbl. Curacao liquer

1. Thinly pare rind from oranges, avoiding white part as much as possible. Finely chop the rind.

2. Section the oranges, squeezing out remaining juice. Combine rind, orange sections and juice, lemon juice, 1/4 cup sugar and the water.

3. Heat to boiling; boil 15 minutes. Cool mixture.

4. Combine remaining 1 cup sugar with the cornstarch. Cream in the butter. Beat in eggs, 1 at a time. Stir in cooled orange mixture and Curacao.

5. Pour mixture into prepared unbaked crust. Roll out top crust on lightly floured surface. Cut out designs or slits for steam to escape.

6. Place top crust on pie. Seal edges with Krimpkut Sealer. Brush egg mixture on crust. Sprinkle with sugar. Bake in preheated 425° oven 10 minutes. Reduce temperature to 350°. Bake 45 minutes longer.

DESSERT PIEROGIS

Pierogi Dough (reference on page 55)

1 cup pureed peach preserves
2 cups pitted fresh cherries
1 can (8 oz.) apricot filling

1. Prepare Pierogi Dough as directed. Fill with one of the above fillings.

2. To cook Pierogi, drop into boiling salted water and cook for 3 to 5 minutes; or deep-fat in oil heated to 360º F. until golden brown. Serve Pierogis with sour cream.

Makes 4 servings.

LUNCH BOX PINEAPPLE CRUSTIES

1/2 cup packed brown sugar
3 tbl. butter, softened
1 pkg. piecrust mix
1/2 tsp. cinnamon
1 can (8 oz.) pineapple chunks, drained well

1. Mix sugar with cinnamon and butter. Make piecrust according to package directions. Roll out on lightly floured surface into 18 x 12 inch rectangle, cut into 3 inch squares with Krimpkut Sealer.

2. Lay 1 pineapple chunk in center of each square; sprinkle with sugar mixture. Bring 4 corners of each square to center. Seal corners with pinching motion. Place on baking sheet. Bake in preheated 425º oven until golden, about 10 minutes.

GERMAN PLUM PASTRY

2 cans (17 oz. each) plums, drained
1 recipe Basic Puff Pastry Dough (reference page 13)
Grated rind of 1/2 lemon
1/4 cup packed brown sugar
3/4 tsp. cinnamon
1 egg white, beaten
Sugar

1. Cut plums in half. Remove pits. Roll out half of dough on lightly floured surface into an 8 x 12 inch rectangle. Fold out remaining dough into same size rectangle.

2. Fold one rectangle in half length-wise. Cut through the folded edge in 3/4 inch strips to within 1/2 inch of the edges.

3. Combine lemon rind, brown sugar and cinnamon. Sprinkle over the plums.

4. Brush pastry edges with cold water. Place cut pastry over half the rectangle. Unfold and fit over remaining rectangle. Seal edges of pastry with Krimpkut Sealer.

5. Brush top of pastry with egg white. Sprinkle generously with sugar. Bake in preheated 425° oven 10 minutes. Reduce temperature to 350°. Bake until golden brown, 25 to 30 minutes. Serve hot or cold.

Makes 4 to 6 servings.

Variation: Substitute sliced fresh peaches for plums, using 1/3 cup brown sugar.

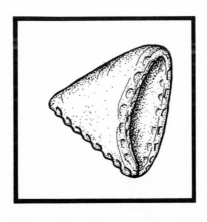

PLUM TURNOVERS

1/2 cup honey
1/3 cup water
2 slices fresh lemon peel
1 cinnamon stick
2 pounds tart black plums, pitted and quartered
1/2 tsp. ground cinnamon
1/4 tsp. ground cloves
2 tsp. cornstarch, dissolved in 3 tbl. cold water
Puff pastry, frozen or (reference page 13)

1. Combine 1/2 cup honey with water, lemon peel and cinnamon stick in large aluminum saucepan and bring to boil over medium-high heat. Reduce heat to medium and simmer 5 minutes.

2. Add plums, cinnamon and cloves and return to boil. Reduce heat to low; simmer stirring occasionally, about 40 minutes. Remove cinnamon stick and lemon peel. Stir in dissolved cornstarch, cook until thickened, about 5 to 8 minutes. Remove from heat and let cool.

3. Roll out pastry on lightly floured surface as thin as possible. Cut into 4 inch squares with Krimpkut Sealer. Place about 1 tablespoon filling in center of pastry. Fold dough over to form a triangle. Place on ungreased baking sheet. Bake at 400° until golden, 15 to 20 minutes.

GROSSMUTTER'S FILLED COOKIES

4 cups sifted all-purpose flour
3 tsp. baking powder
1/4 tsp. salt
1 cup butter or margarine, softened
1 cup sugar
1 egg

Filling:
1-1/4 cups dark raisins, chopped
8 pitted dates, chopped
1/2 cup sugar
1 tsp. flour

1. Sift flour with baking powder and salt; set aside. In a large bowl, beat butter, sugar and egg until mixture is smooth and light. Stir in milk and vanilla. Add flour mixture; stir until well-combined. Refrigerate covered at least 4 hours or overnight.

2. Prepare filling: In small saucepan, combine filling ingredients with 3/4 cup water; mix well. Cook, stirring until thickened, 10 to 15 minutes. Refrigerate until ready to use.

3. Roll out dough half at a time on lightly floured surface to 1/8 inch thickness. Cut into rounds with lightly floured 3 inch Tartmaster. Place rounds 1-1/2 inches apart on ungreased cookie sheets.

4. Place 1 teaspoon filling in center of each round. Top each filled round with a plain round. Seal with Tartmaster. Bake in preheated 350° oven 15 to 18 minutes or until golden brown.

Makes about 3-1/2 dozen cookies.

IRISH SCONES

2 cups sifted all-purpose flour
1 tbl. baking powder
2 tbl. sugar
1/2 tsp. salt
1/2 cup lard or vegetable shortening
1/2 cup currants
1 egg, beaten
1/2 cup heavy cream

1. Sift dry ingredients and place in mixing bowl. Cut in lard with pastry blender until mixture resembles coarse cornmeal. Stir in currants.

2. Make a well in center of mixture. Add egg and milk. Stir until a dough is formed.

3. Turn dough out on lightly floured surface. Knead gently 10 to 15 times. Roll dough into a round to 1/2 inch thickness.

4. Cut into 12 wedges with Krimpkut Sealer. Place wedges on ungreased baking sheet. Bake in preheated 425° oven until golden, 15 to 20 minutes.

NAPOLEONS

1 sheet frozen puff pastry
1 pkg. (3-3/4 oz.) instant chocolate pudding
1 cup sour cream
1/2 cup milk
1 cup confectioners' sugar
About 1 tbl. milk
1 square (1 oz.) semi-sweet chocolate melted with 1 tsp. vegetable shortening

1. Thaw folded pastry sheet 20 minutes; unfold gently; roll on lightly floured surface to 18 x 11 inches. Cut crosswise with Krimpkut Sealer to make 6 rectangles about 3 x 11 inches. Pierce each sheet thoroughly with a fork. Place on ungreased baking sheets. Bake in preheated 350° oven for 18 to 22 minutes. Cool.

2. Prepare pudding according to package directions substituting 1 cup sour cream and 1/2 cup milk for the 2 cups milk called for on the package.

3. For the frosting mix sugar and milk until smooth. Spread on top of 2 of the cooled pastry sheets. To decorate, drizzle chocolate in thin line 1 inch apart, crosswise on frosting. Draw the edge of knife through the chocolate to swirl.

4. Evenly spread half of the pudding on 2 of the remaining pastry sheets. Cover each with a second pastry sheet and spread with remaining pudding. Top with decorated pastry sheets. Refrigerate at least 30 minutes. To serve, cut each pastry with a serrated knife into 6 to 12 equal portions.

Makes about 12 servings.

OLD WORLD BUTTER HORNS

Dough:
4 cups all-purpose flour
1-1/2 cup butter or margarine
1/2 cup sour cream
3 egg yolks
1/2 tsp. salt
1 tsp. vanilla
1 small pkg. yeast

Filling:
1 cup sugar
2 cup finely chopped walnuts or pecans
3 egg whites, stiffly beaten
Confectioners' sugar

1. Crumble yeast into flour. Cut in butter until particles are size of small peas. Add egg yolks, sour cream, salt and vanilla. Mix well.

2. To prepare filling combine sugar, nuts and egg whites.

3. Divide dough in half. Roll each half on board sprinkled lightly with confectioners' sugar into a large circle about 1/8 inch thick. Cut into wedges with Krimpkut Sealer. Heat oven to 400°.

4. Spread each wedge with filling. Roll up starting at wide end. Place on ungreased baking sheets. Bake until golden, about 15 to 20 minutes. Cool. Sprinkle with confectioners' sugar.

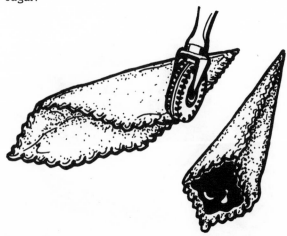

PLAIN CAKE DOUGHNUTS
Without a Hole

4 eggs
2/3 cup sugar
1/3 cup milk
3-1/2 cups sifted all-purpose flour
3/4 tsp. salt
1/2 tsp. nutmeg
1/3 cup melted vegetable shortening
3 tsp. baking powder
1/2 cup sugar
2 tsp. cinnamon
Vegetable oil or shortening for frying

1. Beat eggs until foamy. Add 2/3 cup sugar; beat 5 minutes. Beat in milk and shortening.

2. Sift flour, baking powder, salt, 1 teaspoon of the cinnamon and nutmeg. Add to egg mixture; mix thoroughly. Refrigerate at least 2 hours.

3. Roll out dough on lightly floured surface to 3/8 inch thickness. Cut with floured Tartmaster. Let stand 15 minutes.

4. Heat oil to 375º. Fry doughnuts in oil until brown, turning once. Remove and drain on paper toweling.

5. Combine 1/2 cup sugar and the remaining 1 teaspoon cinnamon in a paper bag. Drop doughnuts in sugar mixture. Shake until coated.

Makes 2 dozen doughnuts.

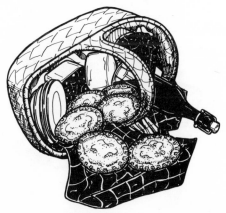

RAVIOLIDOLCI (Sweet)

Pastry Dough:
2 cups all-purpose flour
1/2 cup warm water
1/4 tsp. salt
1/2 cup butter or margarine
Vegetable oil or shortening for frying

Filling:
1 lb. ricotta cheese, sieved
2 eggs
1/4 cup almond paste or 1/2 cup slivered almonds
1 cup applesauce
1/2 cup confectioners' sugar
1 cup light raisins
1 cup cornflake crumbs
Prepare Filling: Combine all ingredients in bowl. Beat until smooth.
Refrigerate while preparing pastry dough.

1. Place flour and salt in mixing bowl. Work in butter with pastry blender until small particles are formed. Add enough water to form a ball of dough that holds together. Knead on well floured board for a few minutes.

2. Roll out dough on lightly floured board to thickness of 1/8 inch. Cut into 4 inch squares. Place 1 tablespoon filling on each square. Fold dough over to form a triangle. Seal edges with Krimpkut Sealer.

3. Heat vegetable oil to 360°. Fry ravioli in hot oil until golden. Drain on paper toweling. Sprinkle with confectioners' sugar and cinnamon.

SOPAIPILLAS

1 cup all-purpose flour
1-1/2 tsp. baking powder
1/4 tsp. salt
1 tbl. vegetable shortening
1/3 cup water
Vegetable oil or shortening for frying
Honey or butter, if desired
Cinnamon and sugar, if desired

1. In medium bowl, stir together flour, baking powder and salt. Cut in 1 tablespoon shortening with pastry blender until mixture resembles coarse cornmeal. Gradually add water, stirring with fork. Turn out on lightly floured board. Knead into smooth ball. Divide in half; let stand 10 minutes.

2. Roll out each half to 10 inch by 12 inch rectangle. Cut into 2 inch by 3 inch rectangles with Krimpkut Sealer. Do not re-roll or patch dough.

3. Heat oil to 375°. Fry 1 to 2 at a time, until golden, about 1 minute on each side. Drain on paper toweling. Serve hot with honey and butter or roll in cinnamon and sugar.

Makes 20.

STUFFED PRUNE PASTRY

Tart Pastry:
1-1/2 cups all-purpose flour
1/2 cup butter, softened
1 egg yolk
2 to 3 tbl. sherry wine or water
1 tbl. sugar
1 tbl. ice water
1/4 tsp. salt

Filling:
1 lb. dried pitted prunes
About 1-1/2 cups sweet white wine
Almond paste

1. Soak prunes in enough wine to cover, overnight. Place prunes and wine in saucepan. Simmer until tender. Cool. Stuff prunes with some of the almond paste.

2. Sift flour sugar and mound on pastry board. Make a well in the center.

3. Place butter, water and egg yolk in well. With one hand, work all ingredients together by working in the flour a little at a time. Add the sherry if necessary.

4. Shape dough into a ball. Cover and refrigerate 1 hour.

5. Roll out tart pastry to thickness of 1/4 inch on lightly floured board. Cut into 3 inch circles.

6. Place 1 filled prune on half of circle. Fold other half over to form a half-moon shape. Seal edges with Krimpkut Sealer.

7. Place on baking sheets. Brush tops with a slightly beaten egg yolk mixed with a little milk. Sprinkle with sugar.

8. Bake in preheated 350° oven until light golden brown, 15 to 20 minutes. Cool slightly before removing from pan. These are delicious served warm or cold.

SWISS NUT TORTE

2/3 cup butter or margarine, softened
2-2/3 cups all-purpose flour
1-1/2 cups sugar
1 beaten egg
2 tsp. rum
1 tsp. finely shredded lemon rind
1 cup heavy cream at room temperature
3 tbl. honey
2 tbl. kirsch
2-3/4 cup coarsely chopped walnuts
1 slightly beaten egg yolk mixed with 1 tbl. milk

1. Beat butter or margarine until light and fluffy. Mix flour, 1/2 cup of the sugar, and a dash of salt. Add to butter; beat until crumbly. Combine whole egg, rum, and lemon rind. Stir into flour mixture until moistened.

2. Divide dough into thirds. Pat 1/3 of dough onto bottom of a 10 inch springform pan. Pat another 1/3 of dough onto sides of pan to a height of 1 inch. On waxed paper, roll remaining dough to 1/4 inch thick rectangle; cover. Refrigerate crust and rolled dough 30 minutes.

3. In skillet, melt the remaining 1 cup sugar over low heat, stirring constantly until golden. Remove from heat; slowly stir in cream. Heat and stir until sugar dissolves. Add honey and kirsch. Stir in nuts. Remove from heat; cool 5 minutes.

4. Spread nut mixture in dough-lined pan. Cut rectangle of dough into 1/2 inch strips with Krimpkut Sealer. Place atop pie in a lattice design. Seal to edges of crust with Krimpkut Sealer. Brush egg yolk mixture over crust. Bake in preheated 350° oven about 40 minutes.

Serves 16.

TORRIJAS

8 to 10 bread slices, about 1/2 to 1 inch thick
1 cup sifted confectioners' sugar
1-1/2 tsp. cinnamon
2 eggs
2 tbl. sherry wine
Vegetable oil or shortening for frying

1. Cut 2 circles from each large slice of bread with a 3 inch round Tartmaster. Mix sugar and cinnamon and set aside. Beat eggs with an electric mixer until lemon-colored. Strain the eggs. Stir in sherry.

2. Dip each bread round into the egg mixture. Fry in 380° oil until lightly browned on each side. Watch carefully as the torrijas brown quickly.

3. Remove from the oil with a slotted spoon and rain on paper toweling. Coat well with sugar mixture. Serve immediately.

Makes 16 to 20 Torrijas

VIENNA TARTS

1/2 cup butter or margarine, softened
1 package (3 oz.) soft cream cheese
1 cup sifted all-purpose flour
About 3 tbl. red currant, rasberry, strawberry or grape jelly
1 egg yolk beaten with 2 tbl. milk
1/4 cup finely chopped nuts
Confectioners' sugar

1. Cream butter and cheese until light. Stir in flour, mixing well. Cover and refrigerate 1 hour.
2. Roll out dough on lightly floured surface into a 12 inch square. With Krimpkut Sealer cut into 2 inch squares. Place about 1/4 tsp. jelly near center of each square. Fold over to form a triangle. Seal with Krimpkut Sealer.
3. Place on ungreased cookie sheets. Brush with egg mixture. Sprinkle with nuts. Bake in preheated 400° oven until golden, 8 to 10 minutes. Cool on wire rack. Sprinkle with confectioners' sugar.

Makes 3 dozen.

Especially For Kids

Easy Recipes for Children to Prepare

JAM BELLIES

A delicious breakfast, snack or light dessert treat.

Jam
White bread
1 egg
Butter for frying

Spoon 1 teaspoon of your favorite jam between 2 slices of white bread. Cut and seal with the Tartmaster. Dip the tart into one beaten egg. Pan-fry in butter until lightly browned. Sprinkle with powdered sugar and serve.

Filling variations-Raisins with cinnamon and sugar, applesauce, blueberries, cherry or other pie filling.

PUPPY TAILS

Hot dog
American cheese, sliced
Whole wheat bread
Oil for frying

Cut off crust of a slice of whole wheat bread using the Krimpkut Sealer. Place slices of hot dog with American cheese on the left side of the bread. Fold the right side over filling to form a rectangle and seal with the Krimpkut Sealer. Deep fry in oil at 365° until golden on each side.

PEANUT BUTTER MUNCHKINS

Peanut butter, smooth or chunky
Raisins
Carrot, grated
Whole wheat bread

Spoon 1 tablespoon of peanut butter on one slice of whole wheat bread. Sprinkle with raisins and grated carrot. Cover with a second slice of bread. Cut and seal with the Tartmaster. Decorate with raisins to make a face. Toast until lightly browned.

BREAD PUFFS

1 cup buttermilk complete pancake mix
3/4 cup water
Swiss cheese, shredded
White bread
Oil for frying

Add 2 cups pancake batter to 3/4 cup water. Stir until mixture is smooth. Set aside. Cut off crust of a slice of a slice of white bread using the Krimpkut Sealer. On one half, spoon shredded Swiss cheese. Fold over to form a triangle and seal with the Krimpkut Sealer. Dip the triangle in the pancake batter coating both sides completely. Deep fry in oil at 365° until golden on each side.

Filling variations-Sliced bananas, grated apples with cinnamon and sugar, jam or preserves.

NOTES

NOTES

NOTES

NOTES

NOTES

NOTES

NOTES

NOTES